TAKING TANGANYIKA

Experiences of an Intelligence Officer
1914–1918

By
CHRISTOPHER J. THORNHILL

Foreword by
FRANCIS BRETT YOUNG

Introduction by
CAPT. S. H. LA FONTAINE, D.S.O., O.B.E., M.C.
Provincial Commissioner, Central Province, Kenya Colony

The Naval & Military Press Ltd

❖

Reproduced by kind permission of the Central Library,
Royal Military Academy, Sandhurst

Published by
The Naval & Military Press Ltd
Unit 10, Ridgewood Industrial Park,
Uckfield, East Sussex,
TN22 5QE England
Tel: +44 (0) 1825 749494
Fax: +44 (0) 1825 765701
www.naval‑military‑press.com

TAKING TANGANYIKA

A COUNCIL OF WAR

General Smuts and some of his Commanding Officers

CONTENTS

CONTENTS

6

LIST OF ILLUSTRATIONS

8 LIST OF ILLUSTRATIONS

INTRODUCTION

by

Captain S. H. La Fontaine, D.S.O., O.B.E., M.C.,

Provincial Commissioner, Central Province,
Kenya Colony.

MANY books have been and are being written about the Great War, and a few about the East African Campaign. So far as I know, however, all dealing with the latter are the works of soldiers who came to East Africa during the War and their experiences are unavoidably coloured by their ignorance of local conditions.

In the reminiscences of Mr. Thornhill, or " Buster Brown " as he was affectionately known by his comrades of the Intelligence Force and East African Mounted Rifles, we have a new and more intimate sidelight thrown upon the Campaign which will make a warm appeal to East Africans. To quote one instance, the episode of the Honeybird is one which some of us could confirm from our own experience.

Here is no attempt at a coherent account of the story of the campaign ; the author is too modest to attempt this, nor do we require it of him. Its value and its attraction lie in the fact that it tells us in simple breezy language, adorned only by a wealth of detail and incident, the story of a typical

9

East African settler soldier during the Campaign which secured German East Africa for the Empire —his joys and his sorrows, his hardships and his diversions, his exploits and his failures. For this reason it fulfils a long-felt want.

Looking back on the Campaign we naturally tend to forget the bitter and remember the sweet; to emphasize the pleasant and gloss over the unpleasant. Mr. Thornhill has told us of both aspects and contrived to invest them with a striking charm and appeal, for which we, his comrades in the Campaign, are very grateful.

FOREWORD

THIS book is the simple, straightforward narrative of the experiences of an Intelligence Officer in the German East African Campaign. That 'sideshow,' now almost forgotten save by those who happened to serve in it, has only produced a slender body of personal documentation. And that seems to me a pity, not only from the literary but also from the military point of view ; for that campaign was unique of its kind : the first tropical warfare waged under modern conditions of transport and armament, and the first in which organized native troops on either side fought with white men and against them : a lamentable circumstance which, now that other nations in Europe have set themselves to the military exploitation of the African native, may be encountered again. The full history of that remarkable adventure, that mobile war conducted in a savage country half as large as Europe, has not yet been written. In any other time it would have been regarded as a major operation. General Smuts, our inspired and inspiring leader, has paid his own tribute to the men who fought under him. " To march day by day," he has written, " and week by week through the African jungle or high grass, in which vision is limited to a few yards, in which danger always lurks yet seldom becomes visible, even when experienced, supplies a test to human nature often in the long run beyond the limits of human endurance. The efforts of all have been beyond praise." And the work of the Intelligence, so truly described at first hand in these pages, was more hazardous and more intolerable to the nerves than any other. I can remember to-day the feelings of relief and of admiration aroused in the men of the First East African Division, held stationary for want of supplies and transport in the shell-raked perimeter camp at M'siha, by the news of the successful exploit of Brown (as we called him) and Lewis and Wienholt in penetrating behind the German lines on the Wami. That was one of the boldest and the most perilous achievements of the whole campaign : a deed of tenacity and daring that will long be remembered. It is described in this book as no more than a series of incidents in the day's work ; and that, I think, gives the measure of this document's value and of the writer's admirable humility. There are no purple patches in it, no exaggerations, no appeals to pity. It is, in short, the narrative, strictly true in detail and atmosphere (as I can vouch from my own experience), of a singularly courageous, observant and good-humoured man ; and the soldier who wants to realize what bush-fighting is like could not find a better text-book.

Francis Brett Young

TAKING TANGANYIKA

CHAPTER I

OUT OF THE BLUE INTO KHAKI

ONE sunny afternoon, August 9th, 1914, I was walking slowly at the head of a small caravan of pack donkeys, attended by a few natives. I say " slowly," for the pace of the East African pack donkey is nothing more than a crawl.

After winding about a rocky path and with difficulty persuading the obstinate pack animals with shoves, pulls and blows to cross a stream, we at last emerged on the flat country covered by the pleasant scented Leshwe bush. The path was a rough one, a mere track made by Somali traders with their camels and cattle trekking down from the Abyssinian border, to barter with the settlers.

We were now almost at our journey's end, after being out of touch with civilization for many weeks. Nearing a post office I had a vague idea about letters which might be waiting for me with news of the outer world, but little knew what a bombshell was in store—news which for the past week had set the civilized world on fire and would entirely change my existence, as well as that of millions of others, for the next few years !

Travelling a few miles on, I came to the crest of a rise and could see in the distance a mere blur of corrugated iron roofs, mingled with gum trees and the familiar red iron tank, marking the presence of a station of the Uganda Railway.

I decided that I could not reach the station before dark as the pack animals were tired, so camped for the night, sending a native on for provisions. The boy returned after several hours, saying that he could not buy the things as the Indian *duka* wanted double the value I had given. I am afraid I here rather lost patience. For one thing, I had been looking forward to having a cup of tea with sugar, an unknown luxury since Louise, one of the pack donkeys, had kicked off her load, which resulted in the tins in the chop-box losing their lids and the contents being violently shaken up with loose curry powder. Even though the cook placidly said it was all right, as with a great deal of sorting he returned each commodity to its own tin in triumph, his tea never tasted the same after that.

So I naturally became rather impatient with Macharia, who now stood before me repeating that the Indian tea and sugar had gone up owing to a *vita* (war) which was on.

" *Vita* ? " said I. " What *vita* are you talking about ? "

" Oh, only a *vita* between the Wazungu."

"A *vita* between the Wazungu! What Wazungu?"

" Oh, only the Wazungu in Ulaya," said Macharia reassuringly. " They are not *vitaring* out here yet, but they might very soon and the Muhindi said he is afraid to sell all his tea and sugar, for if the Wazungu were *vitaring* they could not make any more."

It suddenly dawned upon me that there was really a war on—a real war with fighting. I took up a lantern and have a faint recollection of covering the four miles to the station with the following questions ever passing and repassing through my mind :—

" What war ? "

" It must be a war with Germany—have the Germans landed in England ? "

At last, hot and breathless, I burst into the station-master's office and found him placidly seated with his friends on the floor around a tin of coals, a huge pipe which made a babbling sound being passed from mouth to mouth.

The Indian station-master looked up and I said :—

" What war is this I hear of ? " Then applied the questions which had been circulating through my brain.

After explaining the situation the Indian gave me some old newspapers, which I anxiously read by the station lamp. Midnight found me wending my way back to the tent, cram full of information which seemed almost to deal with events of another age. And all the time, on my way home, I kept on repeating to myself :—

" What, a real war on and I not there ? They are actually fighting ! So wars are not a thing of the Past after all."

I felt I could hardly breathe until I joined something.

It should be mentioned here that I was only eighteen and ideas of war were different then. In fact, I had dreamed of war as a bygone indulgence enjoyed by our forefathers. If nations did fight in this age of civilization, they would only have a few pots at each other and then make peace. I had too often heard men say : " Oh, we are too civilized to fight nowadays." But this very evening I had actually read in the papers that they were fighting like real " good'uns " in Europe.

The next three days I pushed my safari impatiently on, travelling day and night, until we reached Njoro, where I left my animals and equipment at a friend's farm.

I paid off my boys and mounted my trusty little Abyssinian mule. Then with rifle slung on shoulder and cartridge belt round waist, took a short cut across country to Nakuru, where I was sworn in at the District Commissioner's office. Later, having had my mule vetted by the local Veterinary Surgeon, Doherty, we entered a cattle truck, the mule and I, and next day arrived at Nairobi.

On the train was an ex-naval officer going to the capital to enlist, whom I plied with questions all the way. But he was rather inclined to take things seriously and poured cold water on my enthusiasm by saying war was not all " Beer and Skittles."

When we got to Nairobi I saddled Jenny, my mule, and the ride up Government Road was quite a new experience for the little animal. She was a well-meaning little steed, but had never been in a town before—had in fact only recently been brought down from the Abyssinian border, where no such horrors as steam-rollers and cycles existed, to say nothing of cars and motor-cycles, one or two of which might sometimes be seen in the streets of Nairobi in those days.

At last, after a great deal of coaxing and spurring, I got her within sight of Nairobi House ; when suddenly, without warning, from a side street emerged a car, whilst a motor-cycle came spluttering down the road bearing straight for us. This was too much for Jenny's nerves and she took the bit in her mouth and we went full gallop back in the direction we had come, getting half-way to the station before I managed to turn her up a side street and then slowly, by less frequented streets manœuvre my way back to Nairobi House, which was at that time military headquarters.

Nairobi certainly seemed to be flourishing on the war and was fuller and busier than I had ever seen it before. All the settlers in Kenya, then known as British East Africa, seemed to be in the capital. The able-bodied white population had joined up almost to a man, leaving their farms in most cases to the tender mercies of native headmen. There was a war on and farms and property could look after themselves.

I met a man I knew and he told me a camping ground for mounted men had been made on the race-course, a mile away. The numerous men I saw about the streets were stragglers up from camp.

Armed men could be seen riding about in every

B

direction, others dismounted, chatting and joking
about the street corners, bars and shops ; all
apparently killing time until the advance upon
enemy territory should be made.

Every single individual seemed to wear whatever
uniform he pleased, that of the bandolero and
bushranger being by far the most popular ; a wide
awake double terai hat—generally well battered
and slouched—a khaki flannel shirt with sleeves
rolled up and the first trousers or breeches that had
come to hand—the only evidence of uniformity
being the epaulettes pinned or sewn to their
shoulders with cloth lettering denoting the particular unit. Strips of leopard skin adorned the
hats in some cases and coloured silk handkerchiefs
around the neck marked the very dandified. A
revolver or automatic pistol, whether in the shape
of a huge .45 Colt or a small nickle toy, hung
loosely at the hip cowboy fashion from a waistbelt
bristling with rows of cartridges. In addition to
all these arms and encumbrances, some carried
long lances, like the knights of old, only these were
local bamboo and the points were made of soft
iron from the blacksmith's shop. These latter were
" The Lancer Squadron, Lady Monica's Own,"
and were said by some to hold themselves aloof
from the common mounted infantry. Fortunately
when fighting did start the Lancers' officers had
sense enough to make them throw away the sticks,
as the average type of pony then available in the
country was certainly not up to a cavalry charge.

One or two, I noticed, took the war seriously, but
most regarded it as a huge joke. Discipline was lack-

ing, though all were as keen as mustard and itching for the first fight ; which later on accounted for the wonderful achievements of these " Rag-time " soldiers, the East African Mounted Rifles, who, without any training whatever, coming straight from their farms into active warfare, held the German border for many months until regular troops could be got over from India. There were practically no other troops in the country, as most of the King's African Rifles (the native regular army) were many month's safari away fighting on the Abyssinian border. So, except for the Settler's Corps, East Africa was left quite unguarded against the neighbouring German colony, which had a strong force of well-trained troops. Worse still, there were no service rifles and little service ammunition in the country, so the settlers were armed with sporting rifles, while equipment of sorts was hastily manufactured locally.

For some time I stood at the door of Nairobi House, unable to enter for a very noisy and jocular crowd of armed men which filled the entrance hall. At last they came clattering down the steps, a few with brand new flannel shirts under their arms. A man at my side told me that they had been in to draw shirts, but only some lucky ones got them as the others were told their own shirts were still serviceable. He explained that the thing to do when you wanted to draw a shirt, was to wear the oldest one you had.

Most of the troops mounted their waiting mules and ponies, but half a dozen had to walk owing to their mounts having run back to camp. There was a stormy scene between the Sergeant-Major (an ex-regular) and the six muleless troopers. The former insisted that they were to return to camp with the rest of the troop, but the troopers objected to this, saying they must go via the New Stanley Hotel, on urgent business. At last it was decided that the Sergeant-Major should go along with them, just to see that they came home all right.

Now that the entrance of Nairobi House was clear, I hurried in and spoke to the Corporal on guard. He wore the largest spurs I had ever seen and sat with his feet up, surveying his men, most of whom were also lounging about on a bench; but one of them was on guard, and taking it very seriously too, dressed in an officer's tunic cut off at the sleeves and a pair of khaki slacks stuck into mosquito boots. He walked stiffly backwards and forwards, rifle on shoulder, saluting every officer who passed. This was a very unusual thing to do, but the fact that he was an ex-regular captain may have accounted for it and there were not enough commissions to go round at first.

I told the Corporal I had come to join Bowker's Horse.

" What ? You want to join that lot of " stiffs " ? Besides, it is full up. You take my tip and join C Squadron of the E.A.M.R., a really decent crowd of fellows. Come—let me take you along."

And I was hurried off up a flight of steps and pushed into a room where several officers of C Squadron were seated talking seriously over a table.

I pulled myself together and gave them the best

salute I could manage, as I repeated my request to join Bowker's Horse. I was told curtly that it was full up, there were no more mules and I was lucky to join a mounted corps at all. Late-comers like me deserved to be foot-sloggers, but they would try as a special favour to get me into C Squadron, who had a few spare mules.

I said I had my own mount and all equipment. I wanted to serve under Bowker, because he was a hunter like myself, so I should understand his ways of fighting. Besides, I had one or two pals in the corps. This, as I thought, very plausible explanation, only seemed to cause irritation and the officer lost patience and told me curtly that I could not join Bowker's Horse, at the same time producing a form for me to fill in. But just then a middle-aged man of rather powerful build came into the room. His shirt sleeves were rolled up showing his brawny arms, and he had a cap upon his head made of a leopard's mask, the two glaring white fangs of the animal protruding ominously above the wearer's head. He had undoubtedly overheard the conversation, for he said in a booming voice :—

" Who said there was no more room in my corps ? I can do with quite a lot more."

" Captain Bowker ? " I gasped. It might have been a devil dancer ! Was this the man under whom I was so anxious to serve ?

At this the C Squadron captain reminded Bowker of an order the O.C. troops had given, forbidding any more recruits to go to him, as his two squadrons, E and B, had their full complement, while others were not filled. But the old hunter only pooh-

poohed the idea and seizing his legal prey by the arm, led me away to his own office, where I filled in a form.   Then Lieutenant (now Major) Webb went to the ground floor with me and out into the street to inspect my mule and saddle, which he valued and we were all enrolled in the British Army —myself, Jenny, rifle and saddle.   A doubt then seemed to cross his mind and he asked me if I could ride, to which I said I could.   But he was not satisfied until he saw me mount and cross the street, the passing traffic so startling poor Jenny that I had difficulty in getting her back again.   I was then sent off to camp at the race-course, where I was shown a tent by the Sergeant-Major and Jenny was sent out to graze.

CHAPTER II

INTO THE BLUE AGAIN

THAT evening a friend and I went up town to dine and, passing the New Stanley bar, saw a white mule tied up securely to a tree, a great hole having been made by the impatient animal's forehoofs as it pawed the ground, anxiously waiting for its master.

My friend wanted to see someone in the bar—so we both went in, finding it cram full. We saw the six troopers of the runaway mules helping the Sergeant-Major towards the door, all saying fond farewells to friends who were pressing them to stay on. But they insisted that they must look for their mules which had run away that morning—one explaining that a soldier's first consideration was his mount, even if only a mule. With a great deal of clanking of spurs the little body of men made for the door, but as they were about to leave the room some cheery fellow proposed just one more drink, so back three of them came, including the Sergeant-Major.

My friend ordered drinks and we sat in a comfy seat in the corner and I with great interest watched and listened to the talk around us, which was chiefly about the battles we were to fight, how many months it would take us to wipe up the Huns and

so on. At last I noticed our Sergeant-Major friend
and his three remaining troopers again make
valiantly for the door and this time get right outside ; but soon his red face reappeared, asking
generally if anyone had seen a white mule ?

"Who the 'ell has pinched my mule ? Blime,
if I catch the bloke who 'as pinched my mule ! "

"Never mind the mule," said one of his pals.
"Come and have another drink, old fellow. The
mule has only gone to graze."

So it was decided that the mule had gone to graze
and the best place for it too. The subject was dis-
missed, all went back to the bar, and later the
Sergeant-Major, much to the admiration of all
present, gave a demonstration of the latest drill
and bayonet exercises, for which he used the broom
behind the bar. Anyone who could present and
slope arms like that Sergeant-Major was a hero in
those early days.

After dinner my friend and I went on to the
pictures, and as time went on our party gathered
force and at about midnight it took three rickshaws
to cart us back, sitting three and four in a rickshaw.
We left the rickshaws and were walking on to our
lines when suddenly, clear in the night near us,
came the challenge : "Halt ! Who goes there ? "

" —— ! " replied one of our number, saying the
most uncomplimentary thing he could think of.

"Pass friends, all's well ! "

As our lines were at the end of the camp we had
to pass those of several other squadrons and were
challenged in turn by their mule guards, the witty
one amongst us invariably giving some rude retort,

but always receiving the same satisfactory reply:
" Pass friends, all is well ! "

What sort of army is this I have come to ?—I
thought. But later when I myself was on one of
those mule guards, I quite sympathized with the
sentry, for during my watch fully ten persons passed
by, mostly coming from town after a spree, and as
there was no countersign, even if they were in a
condition to give it, it was an impossible job to
examine each individual, so to let them pass was
the only thing to do.

We camped at the race-course, chafing at our
bits for three weary weeks and passing the time
with gymkhanas, sing-songs, boxing matches and
occasional drill. Then one morning E and B
Squadrons, one of which I was in, got their marching
orders. The Germans were trying to break through
at a place near Oldoinyo Narok and we were to
intercept them.

I shall never forget our Squadron Leader
announcing that we were to move and that our
orders were to kill or capture these Huns.

Bowker's Horse entrained for Kiu station, about
fifty miles away—B Squadron going on to Kajiado.

It was evening before we reached Kiu and we
had just time to pitch our tents, frail calico affairs,
known as Porters' tents, which the O.C. had
obtained from a safari outfitter in Nairobi.

The African darkness came down upon us, our
horses were tethered near, and several times during
the night I had to go out and pacify poor little
Jenny, who was much disturbed by the constant
roaring of lions and the moaning and hooting of

hyenas, which persisted in prowling round our camp.

For many who slept behind those thin calico walls this was their first night out in the wilds of Africa and, what was worse, in lion-infested country.

Railways ——
Routes shown thus -----
Scale of Miles
0   50   100   200   300

BELGIAN CONGO

UGANDA

KENYA

To Abyssinia

Kisumu

Gilgil

LAKE VICTORIA
Karungu B.
Kisii
Karungu
Bukoba
Shirati
Magadi
Kajiado
Namanga
Kidongai
LONGIDO
MT KILIMANJARO
MT MERU
Arusha
PARE MTS.
Bwiko
Wilhelmstal (LUSHOTO)
Korogwe
Nairobi
Magadi Junc.
Kiu
Moshi
Tsavo
Voi
Queto
MOMBASA

TANGANYIKA
Ujiji
Tabora
Kondoa Irangi
Mombo
Handeni
Makindu
Turiani
Dodoma
Dakawa
Pangani
ZANZIBAR

LAKE TANGANYIKA

TERRITORY
Magara
Tulo River
Dar es Salaam
Mahoro
Kibata
Kilwa
Narengombie
Kilwa Kisiwani
Mhambia
Lindi

Abercorn

NORTHERN
NYASALAND
LAKE NYASA
RHODESIA
PORT. EAST AFRICA
Ruvuma R.

Many in our ranks were youths straight from office stools in Nairobi, though others were safari-hardened veterans. I could not help admiring some of these city men, who had never ridden a horse before the outbreak of war, about a month ago. In my half-section was one, a boy of about my

own age. I don't know what made us pal up and
become " raggies "—our past lives had been so
entirely different. Fred had lived all his life in
London and had only recently taken up his position
in Nairobi. At the outbreak of war he threw up a
good job and joined the mounted corps, though he
had never been astride a horse before.

Let me describe that first morning out. Fred and I
were riding side by side about the middle of our
patrol, some fifty men. We were following a rough
game track. About two hundred yards ahead was
the Masai guide, walking by the side of the N.C.O.
in charge of the advance guard, which rode in
extended order, fanwise to right and left of him.
We were all riding at ease and in a leisurely manner,
as we did not expect to meet the enemy until the
next day. Fred and I were watching several great
lolloping giraffe and a herd of wildebeest and
zebra, all running before us, throwing up dust as
their hoofs pounded the sun-baked earth. The
morning was cool and the air as clear as crystal ;
a hundred miles away across the border in enemy's
country could be seen the great white dome of
Kilimanjaro, with the sun glistening on its crown.
We were ascending to a waterless gulley when two
rifle shots rang out in quick succession and a
warning cry of " Look out ! Look out ! "

Mules stampeded and all was confusion and—
horror ! There—bearing straight down on the
tangled mass of humanity and horse flesh—was a
great bulk that loomed up in the rising dust like
some primeval monster. Onward it came with the
rapidity of a cavalry charge, straight into the thick

of us. I just had time to say : " Look out, Fred
He is coming this way ! " Then dug in my spurs.
Jenny came to life in a flash and bounded like a
buck. Fred also dug in his spurs, but a surprising
thing happened. *His* mule, too, bounded like a
buck, but he was not in the saddle when it came
to rest on the bank. The rhino ran right over the
prostrate body and I expected to find him trampled
to pulp. But no, those ponderous feet must have
missed him by a hair's breadth, for when the dust
cleared away he sat up—at first a bit dazed—then
grinned and fumbled for a cigarette.

" Well, if that rotten little mule hadn't thrown
me flat, I should have got the blamed thing's horn
right through my middle."

Then he mounted his mule and we both went to
inspect the prostrate monster, which had been shot.

Charging rhino were only to be a feature of this
campaign—we had to get used to them. In time
the men learnt to look out for them and more or
less dodge their cyclonic onslaught ; for nothing
but death will stop a rhino once he takes it into his
head to charge, and it is not always prudent to let
off firearms when enemy patrols are about. That
day I counted no less than eight full-grown rhino
disturbed by our advance, three of which charged
two of them being shot.

Unfortunately Fred was destined to have another
fall very quickly. Immediately we came up, the
dying rhino gave a final snort and kick and our
now excited mules spun round like tops beneath us
and were off like rockets.

Anyone who has not met the Abyssinian mule can

scarcely imagine the alacrity with which these animals can rid themselves of even an experienced rider ; but this little trait and their bad temper generally are more than counterbalanced by their staying power and they will outride any horse in the world where scanty grazing, bad water and prolonged work are the order of the day. Not even the Abyssinian pony, from which they are bred, can stand up to them.

We were now marching almost straight for the white dome of Kilimanjaro, which was across the German border. What romance lay there ! It was the country we hoped soon to conquer. That silent white mountain, lying peacefully bathed in the morning sun, was in sight of all the early fighting, as it could be seen nearly a hundred miles away in the clear highland atmosphere. It was a sinister landmark, always cold and silent, often mocking the wounded when they lay deserted and dying of thirst on those scorched open spaces, gazing towards the distant glaciers of icy water.

We continued our course till midday, when we camped at a muddy puddle used by wandering Masai herdsmen for watering their stock. Though the water was dirty and slimy our mules drank it eagerly. We lunched on bully beef, biscuits and tea. The Masai herdsman told us that the Germans were at a place called Oldoinyo Narok, but this we found was stale news and our skipper half expected to meet them coming through to raid the railway, in which case we might bump into them at any moment. So patrols were sent out in many directions, in the hope of getting in touch with the enemy or at least of hearing more recent news.

Fred and I were sent on one of these patrols and we had a terrific march all day and most of the night, without coming across a drop of water. The next day when we returned, our drinking pools were reduced to a little slime and mud, with a few disconsolate frogs hopping homelessly about. We could not water our animals, so were glad when our O.C. decided to move on in search of a better watering-place. By the middle of the day thirst was becoming intolerable and the patrol which we had accompanied could not go on much longer— the weary animals could barely drag one leg behind the other. Suddenly the man riding in front of me started swearing and beating his poor mule mercilessly.

" Can't you see the road, you fool ? "

And he jagged the poor beast's head violently round. I took little notice of the trooper's bad temper, being so weary and thirsty. Most of us were half asleep, having been riding all night. But suddenly I came to life. There was Jenny also trying to move to the left of the path. I looked in this direction and saw a gully a few hundred yards away—a slight breeze coming straight from it. I knew now that our animals had scented water.

" Come on," I said quietly to Fred and as I gave Jenny her head she went straight for the gully. " Anyway, we will get a drink first, before the stampeding mob come along and muck it up. We'll have the satisfaction of telling the O.C. we have found water."

At the word water a strange light came to Fred's bloodshot eyes, a light I often saw afterwards in the campaign but had never seen before. Fred went down on his stomach and sucked up the precious liquid from a beautiful limpid pool between two rocks, while his mule drank on one side and my mule on the other. There was no holding the animals back—their heads entirely filled the little water-hole and if Fred only knew it, he was in severe danger of having his face crushed in by the mules' feet ; but he heeded nothing and drank on. Then at last he raised his head to gasp and I slipped my water bottle into the vacant place to fill it. The two mules were quite immovable. I started to drink, too, from the water bottle and down went Fred's face again. Suddenly he drew back and spluttering, said :—

" God ! What shall I do ? I've swallowed a young eel or something. Could see it quite plainly swimming about—then suddenly it made a dive for me. No, I haven't swallowed it ! " And Fred put his hand to his mouth. " Wow ! It has got hold of me ! "

And Fred was tugging at a slimy, black, slug-like insect which seemed to have a firm hold on the inside of his mouth and he was apparently in great pain. Soon blood started to flow from his mouth in profusion. It was some time before I realised what had happened.

" Don't tug at it," I said. " It only catches hold with the other end when you get the one end loose and each time it grips it cuts your skin. You've got a leech and if you wait a moment I will get it out for you."

" Won't it crawl down my throat ? " gasped
Fred, blood now trickling down to his tunic.

Though I had never before seen a leech attach
itself to a human being, I had fortunately had
previous experience in getting them out of animals'
mouths and knew that the only way to make them
release their grip was to rub them with salt. So I
made Fred open his mouth and there, securely
fastened by one end to the roof of his mouth and
by the other end to the wall of his throat, was the
unwelcome guest.

" For God's sake don't scare it down my throat !"
—he gurgled, now really in a blue funk. I rubbed
the leech well with salt and without much difficulty
was able to remove it and held it up for Fred to see.

The leech was by now inflated with blood—a
creature about an inch long, dark brown in colour
and thicker than a pencil. When in water it can
swim rapidly, transforming its formidable sucker
into a fish-like tail. In this way it is able to enter
the mouths of thirsty animals and there remain
for days, sucking blood and growing to twice its
normal size, and so tantalizing the beast with pain
that it becomes thin and pines away.

The Masai say that leeches sometimes cause the
death of their animals by adhering to the throat
and so inflaming it that the animal is suffocated.
When the leech has drunk its fill from the animal's
blood it returns to the water, at a convenient
moment, when its host is drinking and in this way
it is able to infect other pools in the neighbourhood.

As I held the loathsome creature between my
fingers, I noticed it was recovering from the effect

CAMPED AT MANGA

[p. 63.

E.A.M.R. GYMKHANA AT BISSEL
A wrestling team ready for action

[p. 108.

FOR WEEKS WE DID CONSTANT PATROLLING

HUNGRY TROOPERS BAG A LESSER KOODU

[p. 6...

of the salt and was endeavouring to grip my finger
with its powerful suckers, so I dropped it hastily.
As it fell on a stone at the edge of the water and
tried to wriggle back, Fred crushed it with his
boot and out squirted a gush of human blood.
With another shudder Fred hastily mounted his
mule and we both galloped off to tell the O.C.
about the water.

We had not far to go as we found the squadron
halted at another larger pool farther up the same
gully, to which the Masai had led them. Tightly
packed round the water were about thirty horsemen,
while others were jostling behind for their turn
to drink. When everyone had drunk his fill, we
moved on to some higher ground and camped under
some thorn trees.

Patrols were again sent out, but this time Fred
and I were detailed for a night picket. Fred was
very pleased at this, as he told me he was beginning
to chafe badly and riding was becoming an agony.
He also felt sore in every limb from his two falls.

" I don't care what work they give me on my
flat feet, so long as they don't ask me to go joggling
through the night on a four-footed animal, me
bumping up and down on two raw patches as big
as half-crowns."

" Why don't you tell the Sergeant-Major and he
will give you a soft job ? "

" What do you take me for ? " said Fred with
meaning in his voice, and I knew that I had offended
my half-section. That he was a novice in the saddle
was evidently a sore point with him and I had not
realized it.

c

All the tents had been left behind at Kiu, and you should have heard the language of some, even old hands, when they heard they were to sleep outside with nothing but the night air between them and prowling lions !

" I don't know what the officers are thinking of. They will lose half a dozen men each night this way ! " said one old veteran, who claimed that he had travelled on safari for fifteen years in lion country and had never before been asked to sleep without a shelter of some sort.

" I call this the frozen limit ! What did the lions do to the railway camps at Tsarvo ? Scoffed a few coolies each night. That's what will happen to us, only worse. The coolies did at least have tents to sleep in."

" A few men taken by the lions each night will soon stop the rozzy war, if our officers aren't more careful."

But alas, what a lot we had to learn before the East African campaign was over. These were only the early days and fortunately for us our enemies across the border knew as little about fighting in lion country as we did. That night each group of sleepers was allowed a huge bonfire, kept going all night to scare off the wild animals—an unheard of and even ludicrous thing in the latter part of the war.

As the half-dozen of us marched out to man the picket the ruddy glow of evening was fading in the west and the men in camp were stoking up their fires. We took up a position about three hundred yards away and ate our meal in silence, as darkness closed around us.

We listened to the occasional whispers of the men as they carried on a disjointed conversation, to the weird bark of the roaming jackal and, far down at the water-hole, the hooting and moaning of the hyena, starting out on his evening prowl. Later, two lions began to roar as they harried a herd of barking zebra, the rumble of whose stampeding hoofs could plainly be heard as the terrified mob charged away into the darkness, possibly leaving behind one of their number to form the feast of the lords of these regions.

Although only one man was to keep watch at a time, so tense was the feeling that none dared to unroll his blanket and thus break the mysterious spell. Again the Kings of the Veldt started to roar, and very much nearer this time. As I sat and listened it was not difficult to guess what were the feelings of the men, with nothing but darkness between them and these terrible killers.

This was an entirely new experience for most of the picket. For even the Sergeant, an old East African settler and a veteran of the Boer War, had never been through anything like it before. In fact, his previous experience with lions was a peculiar one ; he had a taxidermist's shop in Government Road, Nairobi !

I became more and more drowsy as the time went on. I leant comfortably on my saddle, a horse blanket over me. Between spells of sleep and wake-fulness, I listened in desultory manner to the noises of the night and the whisperings of the picket. I felt I wanted to go to sleep badly, but kept on waking—thinking the Sergeant was about to post me for duty. When I was eventually aroused by the Sergeant it must have been midnight, as the moon had risen well above the twisted, gnarled forms of the few scattered thorn trees on our hillock.

What a transformation was there now! In place of the tense darkness and unknown beyond, a fairyland spectacle lay before us. Gleaming in the silvery moonlight the valleys were covered in mist and the hillocks were islands set in seas of opalescent silver. We were on one of these islets and there was our camp, just across the valley, pitched on another. The fires had died down now and the camp was in slumber. Nothing save the distant champing of restless animals could be heard, as they loomed through the mist.

The Sergeant told us that the arrangement had been that each man was to do two hours picket, but as the night was already half gone, he would place two men together on watch. We then drew lots as to the order of our watch.

" No, you don't ! " said the Sergeant sternly, to Fred and me, as we naturally arranged to do our turn together. " One of you has been sleeping through everything, lions and all, so far. When I eventually get some sleep myself, I don't want to be disturbed by a lion licking his chops after a meal off two infant sentries."

I could see poor Fred blush even in the moonlight, at the degradation of our being each paired off with two more worthy veterans. I, too, felt like hiding my head under the saddle blanket, but after a few moments the whole thing only amused me. I knew with my early experience behind me and the way I had come through it, that I was equal to any of them. They merely thought because we were young, we were inexperienced and I tried to put in a word to comfort Fred, but it only seemed to annoy him.

The arrangement now was that when one pair of troopers had done their watch, they were to wake the next. My turn came about the middle of the night, so I went off to sleep again now, knowing I had no need to worry until I was called for duty. But nothing happened and I slept on peacefully until morning. Then I awoke with a start—the picket was preparing to leave.

" What has happened ? " said I to the Sergeant. " Why have they not called me ? "

The Sergeant, strapping up his blankets, said casually : " Oh, I did your spell. Just happened to feel like a little picket myself when your turn came round."

The casual way our Sergeant said this, I know, dropped me to zero in my half-section's estimation, especially as he had been called for his share and this was the very first picket we had done on real active service. I don't know if I was mistaken, but at breakfast I detected just a little coldness in Fred's manner, but this may have been due to the Squadron having been reduced to *posho*[1] and *kongoni*[2] for the menu.

After an early breakfast we started off and I was amongst six men picked by the O.C. to do the advance guard, and as the other five were obviously

[1] Native meal.   [2] Antelope.

exclusively experienced bushmen, I felt that possibly this would raise my prestige with my half-section, whom I had to leave behind to ride in the less worthy place amongst the main body.

We were told to keep a careful watch, as enemy patrols might be about and we expected to run into them at any moment. The six of us rode in extended order, intervals of about ten horse-lengths between, and about three hundred yards in front of the main body, so as to warn it against sudden ambush. I was placed at the extreme left and owing to the nature of the country, was most of the time out of sight of the main body and even occasionally lost touch with the man next to me, when I would hurriedly close in until the bush thinned out again.

We often ran into herds of game and occasionally disturbed a rhino, but there were no signs of the enemy. At midday we halted and with little difficulty killed an antelope, so unafraid were they, and the men cut the hot, quivering flesh from the animal's body and roasted it on the coals. That was about all we had to eat. Even the despised *posho* had practically given out and we had to live on the land, having no commisariat. As one trooper described it afterwards to his anxious mother :—" We lived like lions—ate meat and drank pure water only ! "

But he was wrong ; the water-holes were not always pure, especially just after a herd of zebra or Masai cattle had puddled them up.

The C.O. again sent out patrols to try and get news of the enemy, and as some of them did not get back till late, we had to make up for lost time by travelling at night. About midnight the moon rose and we started off. It was difficult to do extended order advance in such a poor light and we all got badly torn by the " Wait-a-bit " thorns, which had the most devilish claw-like hooks, ripping everything that came into contact with them and so retarding our progress that the C.O. changed our formation and extended us along the track, each man riding at an interval of about fifty yards.

Hour after hour I rode along the winding path, that threaded its way into the semi-darkness, just keeping the man in front visible, the man behind me doing the same, and thus we kept in touch with each other. We halted for about two hours' sleep and then went on again. This time I was in front and rode along in apparent solitude, keeping a wary watch in every direction. As the dawn broke, the path led upwards to rising ground, and then suddenly before me there loomed the unmistakable shape of a tent.

At last, I felt sure, we had come upon an enemy's encampment and I hurriedly passed the word down the chain of horsemen. Then we advanced, only to find the encampment of the District Commissioner of the Masai.

The name of the place was Ol Kononi. We camped there for two days, by a spring at the top of mountain, surrounded by miles and miles of wilderness. The place remains in my memory as the spring of leeches, which we were everlastingly removing from our mules' mouths. During the short stay there Jenny got no less than four huge ones, and it was not an uncommon thing to see a man's mount frothing blood at the mouth.

I joined Fred again, and found that he was in a bad way, but still game. He had developed two painful sores on each buttock and riding was agony. Moreover, the crude diet and bad water were upsetting him, as was the case with many others.

I tried to persuade him to go back to hospital, because there was a chance now as two other men were doing so and later we should be in the Blue again. However, he flatly refused. So whenever we could get away to a quiet place, or at night, I did my best to bathe his wounds. He had got them in an awful state, as his riding-breeches adhered to the sore places each time we rode and were painfully torn away whenever he dismounted, so they became inflamed and festered ulcers. He refused to tell the Sergeant-Major, in case he should be sent back and so miss the fighting. I think in some of those long forced marches Fred almost deserved a V.C. for his bravery, and I believe I was the only one who knew his sufferings. All through the long night marches he would stand up in his stirrups, or walk at his mule's side, but he could not always thus evade sitting on his saddle. At times I thought of reporting his condition for his own sake, but as we had no doctor or even dresser, and, worse still, no medicines of any sort, I thought it would make little difference, especially as he could not now return to Headquarters.

The District Commissioner reported that a small force of Germans had crossed the border, but had returned again. Our O.C., thinking that this might be a scouting party for a larger invasion, decided to join up with B Squadron, who were reported to be near the German border. So all the next day and most of the following night we rode onwards until we got in touch with B Squadron at the Manga River.

We found them in a worse plight than ourselves for rations. We were able to give them a little coffee and maize meal we had procured at Ol Kononi, but only enough for one meal. The joy with which they received these humble offerings was almost unbelievable, as they were living exclusively on venision and water.

After patrolling the border for some days in the vicinity of Longido, we marched back to Kajiado, the nearest railway station.

A wily Goanese by the name of Nazereth, expecting the E.A.M.R. would be pretty dry when they returned from the chase, had already opened a wet and dry canteen at Kajiado and the men simply revelled all day and up till midnight, when we received the news that the Huns were about to attack Kisii and then make for Kisumu. A long train had therefore just run into the station to take us down to the lake to save Kisumu.

Everyone was astir in an instant, or, rather, those who could move—others being carried by their pals. So in the end all got safely aboard the train and by dawn we found ourselves steaming full speed on the way to the lake. Our ponies and mules had been left behind, but these were to come on by the next train.

" This is bliss," said Fred, lying on his belly on a

hard iron cattle truck and watching the landscape
glide by. " I don't want to see my mule for a long
time. Do you think there is any chance of them
getting lost or pinched ? "

As we had not up to the present been issued with
rations, there was very little food on board and we
were famishing. The small wayside refreshment
rooms could not cope with such a host and were
overwhelmed—the Goanese steward and his staff
looking on helplessly as dishes were snatched from
their hands and greedily devoured without cere-
mony, while his larder was looted. Even so, half
of us got nothing at all ; but we were promised a
square meal when we got to Nakuru and a wire
was sent ahead.

All were famishing, some of us not having had a
morsel to eat since morning, and we therefore made
a mad rush for the hotel when the train arrived.
Everyone ran his fastest in case he should not get
a place to sit down and the road between the station
and hotel was filled with men running as if for dear
life, while the natives and other inhabitants stood
aside, staring in wonderment at the behaviour of
so many " Wazungu."

The large dining-room was filled with starving
men and still more came, who had to wait for the
second relay. At last all were fed and the train
moved on.

CHAPTER III

THE FIRST ENGAGEMENT

ON arriving at Kisumu we boarded the S.S *Clement Hill,* while our horses were to come on by the S.S. *Sibyl.*

We steamed up the Kavirondo Gulf in the direction of Karungu Bay, where the Germans were reported to have crossed the border. We had taken plenty of provisions on board with us this time and everyone was in the highest of spirits. As our steamer glided over the rippling blue waters of Lake Victoria we passed the time playing cards, lolling about the deck or going to admire the cannon, which was the pride of every man's heart.

Yes, we actually had a cannon on board ! It may not have been the latest model, yet it was a cannon ! Or rather, to be quite truthful, a one-pounder French Hotchkiss, made, as one over critical fellow observed, in the year 1888. But to me and others who knew nothing of artillery, it was the most wonderful gun and was besides, our own ! It was proudly placed on the raised deck of the forecastle.

By afternoon most of the men had grown tired of admiring the cannon and I went up to her and was caressingly touching one of the wheels, which I remember had been newly painted, when I was

told gruffly by some approaching men to make
room for Admiral Nelson and his men, and on
looking round I saw four B Squadron fellows, the
foremost wearing a cocked hat and many rows of
medals cut out of cigarette tin lids, and the two
last standing rigidly to attention with ship's brooms
in their hands.

Nelson—who looked more like Von Turps, being
tall with two weeks' growth on his chin—his cocked
hat set well back, his foot resting on a packing-case,
his rows of tin medals glistening in the sunlight—
pompously scanned the horizon with a telescope
(in reality an empty ginger beer bottle). At last he
lowered it and said, pointing with a flourish :—

" Do you see that Hun Dreadnought over there,
Master Gunner ? "

" Aye, aye, sir ! A floating hot-bed of square-
heads ! "

" Then sink it, my man ! Sink it to the very
bottom of the ocean ! "

The gunner clapped his eye to the sights of our
Hotchkiss, his fingers fumbling with the mechanism,
and at last there issued from within a loud click,
with wonderful livening effects to the others. The
Admiral clapped the gunner on the back, saying :—

" Well hit, my man ! Well hit ! You got her
fair and square amidships."

At the same time the two figures with brooms
now each in turn, with great violence, started
ramming the broom handles up the muzzle. I
don't know which they thought they were doing—
ramming home a fresh charge, or cleaning the gun.
At a sign from the Admiral they smartly saluted

simultaneously, and, with a click of the spurs, again were two rigid figures, brooms in hand, on either side of the cannon mouth. Here the gunner was preparing for a second shot when the Admiral signed to him to wait and walked up to one of the rigid figures, accusing him of having his shirt on and explaining that it was an unknown thing in the history of brave British seamen for a man to fire his gun with his shirt on.

" Wretched knave ! Take the filthy thing off immediately ! "

At this the gunner rather reluctantly removed his shirt, while his companion continued to stand motionless to attention. Then another shot was about to be fired, when the gunner exclaimed that a man without his shirt put him off his shot, and he would not have it, as the sun reflected from the man's white body to the sights. At this the Admiral went up to the shirtless offender, saying he would be court-martialled for letting his chest slip to his stomach, and besides, could he not see the light shining straight from it on to the gun ? The Admiral here received the dirty broom full in the face. Then they all sat down by the gun and sang pirate songs and sea shanties.

About half an hour later found us nearing Karungu Bay. We were all lined up on deck receiving a day's rations, as about a hundred of us had been given orders to land immediately anchor was weighed and hunt down the parcel of Huns who were reported to be in the neighbourhood.

As I was standing in the queue ready with my haversack and nose bag to receive rations I heard

the following conversation between an officer and
some N.C.O.'s regarding the German colours now
flying on Karungu Hill, half a mile to our left.

"So it is only 'bibi's' clothes hung on a pole?
But why should she hang them there?"

"They say she got hysterics about the Germans,
so is signalling for help."

"But don't you know it might be a German flag
and that they have taken Karungu Bay?"

"I don't know."

Boom! The conversation was cut short by a
shell screaming over our heads, fired from some
unseen field-piece hidden on the shore.

Just then a small German steam-boat, the
Mwansa, glided from her hiding-place amongst the
papyrus and let us have it in quick succession from
her three pompoms. Thus the din went on.
Boom! Boom! from the nine-pounder, and Pop,
Pop! from the savage little pompoms, sending up
little spurts of angry spray all around us. Then a
burst of machine-gun fire drilled neat rows of
holes along the wooden awnings a few feet above
our heads.

We were "in it" at last! But now it had come
it seemed to lose all the romance.

It was obvious that we had fallen into an ambush
cunningly laid and one hit only from any of those
guns at our water-level would send us to the bottom.
The S.S. *Winifred*, though a comparatively large
cargo boat, had very thin plate, which did not
seem more than a quarter of an inch.

The fire from the German nine-pounder was
improving and they succeeded in bursting a shell

right overhead, the shrapnel rattling on our decks. The next shot was a fair hit, striking us in the woodwork just where the funnel joins the ship, blowing a hole four feet in diameter. Another of these a little lower would sink us, but the Germans had made the great mistake of trying to be too sure, holding their fire too long and so bringing themselves within our rifle range. Our quick and accurate reply with rifle fire was beginning to unnerve the gunners and they secured no more hits, for if we could not drill and salute, most of us did know how to shoot. We lay down upon the deck, taking what cover we could and firing volley after volley at the enemy who were some fifteen hundred yards away.

Immediately the first shell was fired, the Skipper did the most sensible thing possible, which was to turn the boat head on for open water and go full steam ahead. Before the Germans could recover from the effect of the hail of bullets, we were carried to safety.

But what was our cannon doing all this time? Why has the cannon been left out?

I, personally, was too occupied to notice all its crew's movements during the first part of the fight; but from hasty glances from the corner of my eye and stories that I heard afterwards I can give the following account, which I think is fairly accurate.

As you will remember, the cannon was placed on a little raised deck in front of the bridge on the fore-castle. As soon as the first enemy shot was fired, a crew, which had been previously told off for the purpose, rushed to their posts at the gun, only to

find the lock out of order. This, however, was
fairly speedily adjusted and a shell fired. But by
now our boat was turning round and the bridge
was between the gun and the enemy, putting the
gun out of action. Nothing daunted, the crew
cried for volunteers and between them they hoisted
it bodily over the bridge. Then, when the gun
had at last reached its new position at the extreme
end of the after part of the ship, it was found that
the top bar of the rail, a thick iron one, came just
in front of the muzzle ; so a mound of biscuit tins,
whisky cases and other provisions was piled up
and on top of this platform the gun was placed,
now clearing the rail. But just as the gunner was
about to fire, an empty biscuit tin crumpled in
and the whole structure gave way, upsetting the
gun and crew, the shot going miles in the air. Still
the valiant crew were not to be done out of another
shot at the enemy, and a Lance-Corporal named
Mercer had an idea. He rushed down to the engine-
room, collared the engineer's hack-saw and laboriously cut through the iron rail, so enabling the little
gun to poke her nose clear from obstacles. The
fight, however, was over by now, and here I
remember having time to look round. There was
our little cannon poking her wicked nose clear of
the rail, seeming to say :—

" Where are they ? Which are they ? Just let
me get at them ! "

But, alas, the enemy were now far out of sight
and range. Yet the gun crew did let off one shot
into the blue, which was greeted with loud cheers
from all around.

Our Skipper steamed on as if the whole German navy was at our heels, till at last night set in and we came to a standstill amongst a maze of papyrus covered islands. All lights were forbidden and a careful watch was kept, lest the S.S. *Mwansa* with its superior guns should follow up and sink us.

Later it was whispered that the *Mwansa* was stealing down upon us. The night was cloudy and pitch black, but sure enough there was the German ship, silently creeping round us and we felt that it would open fire at any moment. Silence reigned and the feeling was tense, when clear on the night air came the hail :—

" What ship is that ? "

" The *Winifred*. Who are you ? "

" The *Kavirondo*."

" Liars ! Liars ! " whispered a trooper at my side, as we levelled out rifles in readiness at the blurred object in the dark.

" They may sink us amongst the crocodiles, but we shall have a whack at them before we go down ! " said another.

" Trying to fool us, are they ? Not so easy my square-headed friends," chipped in a third.

Just then our Sergeant-Major, rebuking us for so much noise, said the word had been passed on from the O.C. that we were about to attack the German vessel by running alongside, all hands leaping on board and overpowering the enemy. Their boat being a small one, we could soon do this by sheer weight of numbers.

The password was " Entebbe," that is to say that when grappling with a man in the dark, should he

D

whisper " Entebbe " in your ear, you were to spare him ; but if he refused to say this magic word, you were to throttle, knife or drown him. Some of the men had pocket knives, a few had ' Bushman's Friends ' and half a dozen murderous looking butcher knives were brought up from the cook's galley. I remember one of these being thrust into my hand and I kept it for many months afterwards as a souvenir. No firearms were to be used whatsoever, as they were too dangerous and likely to do damage to our own side in such a scrimmage. Other men were told off to be prepared with ropes to lash the enemy's boat to ours immediately we came together.

" Show your lights *Winifred,*" came the cry from the darkness.

" You show us yours," returned our Skipper.

" Show our lights for you to see where to bust our boilers ? No b—— fear ! " muttered the irrepressible trooper at my side.

Then our enemy threatened to put a shot through us if we did not show our lights immediately, so the Skipper turned on his lights, but only for the fraction of a second.

" Not long enough," protested the man on the other boat. " We can't see anything."

" No, I am damned if we turn them on longer for you to get your sights on us," again exploded the trooper. " Take my word, Skipper, and don't you let them fool you. You just run us alongside, Skipper, and we'll show you how to throttle a Hun. He won't be able to say " Entebbe," or anything else, if I get my mits on his throat."

" Shut up, you fool ! You are giving the password away," growled the Sergeant-Major in a threatening whisper, and the trooper himself was wellnigh throttled.

After some more hailing in the dark between the ship's officers, it was decided that each side should send out a small boat to arbitrate. This was done and we found that our suspected enemy was the tug *Kavirondo*, a British boat about the same size as the *Mwansa* and carrying the only effective gun on the lake. This boat, I heard afterwards, should have co-operated with us in the engagement at Karungu, in which case we should have probably captured the whole party of Germans and their boat ; but these well-laid plans were upset by the officer in charge of the *Kavirondo* being too zealous. For instead of making arrangements to co-operate with us at once, he first went to the port of Mwansa and, on his own, bombarded the town and only then came on to keep his appointment, arriving at Karungu hours late, to find that the battle had been fought and both the attackers and the attacked had fled in different directions.

As navigating the lake with a comparatively large boat like the *Winifred* was dangerous after dark, the two boats anchored for the night and at dawn returned to Karungu Bay, where we landed and were informed by the natives that the Germans had evacuated the place, making for the port of Mwansa immediately the fight was over. The enemy had also taken with them their dead and wounded.

Grunts of satisfaction were heard from our men at this information, and we now felt that we were the victors. Our Squadron Poet, Lance-Corporal Squires, got up quite a dashing poem about the fight, not forgetting to emphasize the fact that we were both soldiers and sailors too and bequeathing upon us the new title of "Bowker's Horse Marines ! " Bursts of this song could be heard all day long, though I have quite forgotten the words now.

CHAPTER IV

SOLDIERS AFLOAT

A FEW hours later the S.S. *Sibyl*, sister ship to the *Winifred*, arrived and anchored alongside with our horses on board. They seemed to feel the heat intensely. I remember seeing Jenny, my poor little mule, head and ears drooping, squeezed in between a lot of great fat ponies, and I took the first opportunity later to take her across a biscuit and also draw up from the lake a bucket of water. She drank it almost at a gulp and whinnied for more. I can't think why the men left in charge of the mounts could not give them all sufficient to drink, when they were surrounded by miles and miles of beautiful fresh, cool water.

On returning to the *Winifred*, I was told off amongst a party to cut grass on shore for the animals. Three boats were lowered and as ours touched the surface the water started bubbling and pouring in through half a dozen holes in the bottom, made by machine-gun fire. These we at last managed to plug up with twisted fragments of rope. Then, when all was ready, the Corporal in charge of the respective boats proposed a regatta, so we set off at full speed, all straining at the oars. But no matter how we bent our oars, our particular boat seemed to make very little headway, the trouble being that we were a lot of " land lubbers," as we were told by the other boats—and were left far behind, while sweat poured from our brows.

One of the crew expressed a desire to board the *Kavirondo*, lying only a little out of our course, to see the best naval gun on the lake, about which we had heard so much. Besides having bombarded Mwansa, it had only four days ago sunk a German dhow at a mile range—little less than a miraculous performance to us. Oh, if it had only been with us at the battle of Karungu Bay ! What prizes might we not have won !

" A steam tug, a nine-pounder, three pompoms and a machine-gun ! " counted up the cox of the boat.

We were soon alongside the *Kavirondo* and hoisted ourselves up by the anchor chain. The white officer was away and the deck was in charge of a few black sailors, so we had the run of it. The gun was right forward and, as our Corporal explained, it was a proper naval gun because it had no wheels, but was merely mounted on a moving swivel arrangement attached to a strong iron frame bolted to the wooden deck, enabling the muzzle to be pointed in any direction, which was a great advantage as we had just learnt in the fight. But we were rather taken aback to see that it was only a muzzle-loader, i.e.—the shell as well as the powder had to be rammed down from the muzzle and the piece discharged by means of a match applied to a touch-hole !

This, with our one-pound Hotchkiss, was all the

artillery available to defend the shipping on the broad waters of Victoria Nyanza at the outbreak of war.

After feasting our eyes on the gun for some time, we again slid down the anchor chain—much, I think, to the relief of the native crew. Our Corporal, although he may not have known much about guns, I must certainly admit had an eye for country and soon spotted a green patch of grass about half a mile beyond where the first two boats were landed. He explained that his eye was accustomed to looking out for good grazing as he had a sheep farm.

" There is a native village near by, which would come in handy for our labour supply," he further mentioned.

The crews of the two other boats, we noticed, were laboriously cutting the grass themselves, whereas our leader declared, to our entire satisfaction, that he would not have the hands of his men soiled by manual labour, which was a nigger's job.

Our boat was brought to a standstill at the shore by bumping against a jagged rock. Everyone was upset, but managed to scramble out none the worse for the shaking and tie the boat up securely. A swell was on and each time she rose and fell the bottom bumped violently against the rocks in the water.

" Don't you think the bottom may be smashed through ? " anxiously enquired one of the troopers.

" No fear ! These boats are strong—I know them. Our portable dipping tank at the farm is made of exactly the same material," replied the Corporal.

We then surrounded the village and herded down
the inmates in a drove—some twenty men, women
and children—none of whom, by the way, wore a
stitch of clothing. The women, however, besides a
string of beads around their waists, had a miniature
horse tail hanging behind, suspended from the
waist.   Some of the men had hippo and boars
tusks hung from the neck. The Chief, a very old
man, but still possessing a remarkably fine physique,
had a very frayed and worn leopard skin hanging
from his shoulders, evidently a relic of his youthful
hunting activities.   In his hand he held a huge
broad bladed spear.

However, in spite of their peculiar get-up, these
people cut grass for us willingly and soon we had
sufficient to fill the boat, returning to it just in time,
for the rock was now beginning to enlarge the small
crack the pounding had made.   The Chief, on
seeing this, came to our rescue by sending one of
his young men for a substance like mud, which he
explained his people put in the cracks of their dug-
out canoes ; and we certainly found it most efficient
as it completely stopped the flow of water. The
Chief then applied some to the bullet holes at the
bottom of the boat, saying with a disapproving
shake of his head :—

" Germanie, mbaya ! Marag, marag ! "

We were about to leave when the old man asked
us to wait, as his son, Odiano, had been sent for,
and he would like to talk to us through the young
man's interpretation.

Odiano, we learned, had been to a Mission School

and could speak both English and Swahili, as well as Kavirondo.

The old Chief, in his broken Swahili, asked us about the war and expressed his wish to help fight the Germans, if the English would give him guns and half the cattle loot. He had heard that the Government had given part of the loot to native levees who helped to fight the Nandi and Sotik some years back. He asked our Corporal what his big Chief's name was, and on being told that it was King George, he exclaimed :—

" Oh, yes, Kingee Georgee. I know Georgee, he is on the rupees and certainly is a big Muzungu, only the Munhindi shopkeeper tries to make out he is a Muhindi (Indian) like himself. Hence all money comes from India. But I know better ! For do not some Muzungu also have beards ? Anyone could tell the difference between a Muzungu's beard and a Muhindi's."

He then asked our Corporal to write a letter to ' Kingee Georgee ' putting forward his proposition, not forgetting the rifles and the share in the cattle. This the Corporal solemnly promised to do.

Here the Chief turned round and said his son, Odiano, was coming and we saw a young man running swiftly towards us over the brow of a hill. On drawing near he slackened his pace and we took in the details of his dress. He was tall and well made like his father. Upon his head he wore a brand new double terai hat with a scarlet band from which rose a long, white ostrich feather and around his neck was a speckled blue silk handker-chief, but below this the eye met nothing more than

Nature's brown skin, until we came to a gay pair of check golf hose and finally a highly polished pair of tight brogue shoes. This was all he had on with the exception of a string of shiny brass beads around his waist and brass wire bracelets on his arms. This was a typical native of the lake shores, emerging into civilization.

As the young man arrived breathlessly he clicked his heels smartly and saluted us each respectfully in turn, saying : " Goodee morning, Sah ! " Then listening intently to what his father had to say, he turned to us again and said :—

" Gentlemen, my father, he says he feel most graceful to having privileged for cutting grass for Kingee Georgee's pundas." Here the Corporal interrupted to hurriedly thank the Chief and then said to us :—

" Come away, come away ! We must be getting along." And with this we pushed our boat off and arrived at the *Sibyl* an hour before the other boats, whose crews came in hot and tired with only half a load of grass each, which they had laboriously cut with their own hands.

That evening we had a jolly old sing-song on board, when a lot of quite good Bush talent was exhibited. The next day all the boats steamed out of harbour early in the morning, the *Kavirondo* returning to patrol the German waters of the lake and the *Winifred* and *Sibyl* taking us back to Kisumu. We heard that the Germans had again been seen in the vicinity of Oldoinyo Narok, so we were to go back to Kajiado.

We arrived at Kisumu in the afternoon and as

most of the men dashed off up town as soon as the boat touched the pier, it was decided to unload our goods the following morning ; but a few of the provisions were off-loaded and stacked on the quay at the ship's side. The O.C. arranged for a guard of three men and a sergeant to be placed over the provisions before he also went to dine up town.

Fred and I were on this guard and, after our Sergeant had arranged as to what hours we were in turn to take duty, he left us, saying he was also dining up town and, should he not get back, we must simply wake the next man when our time was over.

We made our beds down on the deck to get a few hours' sleep before our turn came and were just dropping off when two old soldiers came along and started chatting about the fight, telling us tales of the Boer War and making themselves very pleasant generally. Then by accident they found we were both on guard that night, at which they expressed their indignation at our officer's putting the two youngest men in the Squadron on duty, while they and everybody else were enjoying themselves up town.

" It is a downright shame," said one. " It grieves my heart at the injustice ! Why, I have a good mind to help the youngsters myself and so let them have their sleep, for they are after all only growing boys and need it. I tell you what, Alec—supposing we each did the guard for the two kids, if they promise in return to give us their whisky rations to-morrow evening ? How would that suit you ? "

"Horace, it's a go!—I am game. We, with experience, must help the young and inexperienced. Horace, you have more kindness in you than I thought. Why—it is the very thing I thought of doing myself."

"But," I protested, " I am afraid I can't do this as I have bartered to-morrow's tot with Murphy for a pot of jam."

"Well, the one after that, then," said Alec.

"And that one I have bartered with Bill for a packet of cigarettes."

"The devil you have! And what have you bartered the one first day in next year for? A box of matches, I suppose? Are there any tots vacant at all?"

"Yes—the next after the next, and you may have it."

"Right, that is fixed. And what about you, Fred?"

Fred, who was also a teetotaller, said his tot was only booked for one day and Alec could have the one after that.

"But," said I, " is it right for a soldier to barter his duties with rations in this way?"

"Right? Of course it is right and legal. Don't I know? Have I been in the army twenty years for nothing? Is that not right, Alec?"

Alec replied that he had also been through the Boer War and knew it to be absolutely legal and right; and we young fellows should not try and teach old soldiers their business.

So it thus ended that the two old soldiers took over our duties, and as we were really tired after all the late excitement, we settled down to a good night's rest. The last thing I heard before going off to sleep was Fred's drowsy voice at my side saying :—

" I am so glad we let them do the guards—they are old regulars and know their job all right. I wonder if we shall ever get to like picket as they do ? We have done quite a lot of them now and I'd sooner have my night's rest any time."

The next morning the camp was in an uproar. Someone had stolen two cases of Johnny Walker from the Quartermaster's store. The E.A.M.R. always carried with them several cases of Scotch whisky, as it was claimed that settlers were used to their whisky tot at night and they said they simply could not fight without it ! Thus it had become our daily ration and never on any account was it left behind, no matter what provisions had to be sacrificed.

" What had the guard been doing ? What the devil had the guard been doing ? " was the question repeated everywhere. Soon the Sergeant, Freddy and myself with another trooper were hauled up before the officer and little by little the whole story leaked out. So the court martial broke up and we all joined forces to search for Horace and Alec. The former was eventually found stowed away down an empty cargo hole, with an array of water bottles—some still filled with spirits—hanging round his neck. Alec was also unearthed—well hung with water bottles. These bottles, it was found, had indiscriminately been taken from sleeping comrades and filled up with spirits.

The anger of our officers was here diverted from us to the old soldiers who were given four extra mule guards each ! While Fred and I got off with a severe reprimand.

Punishments were very light in the Settler's Corps in those early days. Everyone was so keen to win the War and do his bit that there was seldom room for serious misdemeanour.

CHAPTER V

ON THE BORDER

THAT afternoon we boarded a train for Kajiado and during the day we heard that the New Stanley Hotel at Nairobi had invited the whole of our Corps to dine that evening. Our Officers had replied that we should be passing Nairobi in the early hours of the morning, so then we were invited to breakfast instead.

We arrived at the station at about 7 a.m. and marched up to the New Stanley, our force some 120 in all, stacked rifles and equipment in the lounge and then sat down to a really good breakfast in the big dining-room, while an Italian band up in the gallery played " It's a Long, Long Way to Tipperary."

" It makes you feel like conquering heroes returning from battle," said a man at my side.

" Anyway, we have been in the first real fight in the country," said another proudly.

When we could not possibly eat any more bacon, eggs and sausages we hurried back to the waiting train and continued our journey to Kajiado. We then rode out to Kidongai, about fifty miles away, and after staying there for some weeks, eventually went on up to the German border and camped at Manga, at the foot of Oldoinyo Narok.

For weeks we did constant patrolling but saw very little of the Germans, as they kept to their stronghold—Longido.

The war to us out here seemed everything and of all importance, although we did realize that in Flanders it was raging far more fiercely and was deciding the fate of the world. Up to the present we had not done much, but we hoped soon to see some stiff fighting when we were strong enough to invade the enemy's country. You can imagine, therefore, our feelings when we were told that the Governor of the Colony, in reply to his enquiry, had received orders to the following effect from the War Office :—

" Defend your country, if you think it worth while ! "

" Why, they don't seem to think we have a war on out here at all and that the country is no damned use ! " said one old and indignant settler, who had spent all his capital and half his life battling the wilds and making it a place secure for himself and his family.

I suppose the fact is that nobody at home had much time to think about East Africa in the crisis of the first few months, so we simply had to rub along as best we could, using what little local resources were available.

We had orders not to enter German territory and our duties were merely to keep an eye on any movements of the enemy. One day a few mounted men out patrolling noticed a body of German infantry well armed with machine-guns, marching for our supply depot, Bissel River. They saw the

DESTROYED RAILWAY BRIDGE

[p. 69.

GERMAN PRISONERS OF WAR

[p. 69.

STATUE OF GERMAN GENERAL IN TANGA

[p. 39.

Germans first without being seen themselves, so quickly followed, taking cover from the low trees and grass ; and, when they were near enough, opened fire suddenly from the rear. The Germans were the first to fall and were thrown into confusion, but later got down to fighting and drove off the handful of attackers. The sad part about this skirmish—known as Ingedo Hill—was that four of our men, who had been left behind helpless and wounded, were stripped of their clothing, bayoneted and mutilated by the enemy.

The Germans never tried to break through again and the next engagement was when we attacked their stronghold. This took place some time afterwards and by then there were in the country a certain number of Indian native troops—a few of them regulars, but mostly State troops.

On the afternoon before the day of the big attack, our men left the camp at Manga River and travelled on until dark, rested until midnight and then pushed on again to surprise the enemy at dawn. Bowker's Horse, still so called although Captain Bowker had now left us (we were really E.A.M.R.), marched and reconnoitred all night—our orders being to get right at the back of the enemy's position to cut them off should they want to retreat to Arusha. At dawn we were to attack the position in conjunction with other troops on the opposite side of the mountain. But, just at the critical moment, our guide did not seem quite sure of his ground and took us on beyond the German lines, so we had to return. The sun had already risen before the first shot was fired. We had hoped to

E

surprise the enemy, but they had got news of our coming, so there was nothing left but to advance in the open. The Germans were quite ready for us and had taken up a good position at the foot of the mountain. They opened fire on our approaching ranks and we in reply lost no time in getting into the best position we could find and returning fire. They also had the advantage of seeing us take up our position, whereas they themselves were hidden behind trees, boulders, bushes and grass which grew everywhere at the foot of the mountain, and we did not know precisely where to fire. Most of our men seemed to think the deadly gun fire was coming from the mountain-side and so shot high and over the heads of the enemy, who were actually concealed at the foot of the mountain, only some eighty yards away. We were getting decidedly the worst of it, but hung on for several hours, as we now distinctly heard our main force's mule battery booming away in the distance on the other side of the mountain.

Towards midday our C.O., getting news that the main attacking force did not seem to be making headway and as we were losing men constantly through hidden snipers, decided to retire until out of range of the mountain, where we off-saddled and rested our animals, at the same time keeping a watch should the Germans try and break back to Arusha. Later on we received word from the Commanding Officer on the other side of the mountain that the assualt was a failure and we were to retire to Manga. Our little party had suffered considerably the worst of all the attackers, our losses out of a total of 120 men being ten killed and some half-dozen wounded. The combined numbers of the other units—some 900—only lost one killed and one wounded. We felt our losses all the more as almost all these men were old and well-known settlers, or their sons—men in most cases who had been closely associated with the early development of the country.

Although I don't think we did very much damage to the enemy, we certainly " put the wind up them," as our Skipper expressed it. They left their stronghold next day, retiring over the dry belt to Kamfontein, a fortified position many miles across the border, and our forces occupied the vacant stronghold of Longido mountain.

CHAPTER VI

THE TALE OF TANGA

AFTER this there followed many weary months of stagnation, our advance posts now being Longido, Manga and Lone Hill, while the German posts were Kamfontein, at the foot of Mt. Meru, and Ngasari, Ngare Nyuki, Ngari Nairobi and other outposts on the foothills of Kilimanjaro. Between these outposts was a dry waste some sixty miles broad which was "No-man's-land" and patrolled regularly by both parties.

Life in these days was humdrum and uneventful —constant patrols and constant watching over dry, arid, waterless country—the only break in the monotony being when the patrols of opposite sides occasionally met in "No-man's-land." Then a sharp skirmish generally took place, followed by the hasty retreat of the side which had been so unfortunate as to see their opponent last.

The great secret in this type of Bush warfare is to see your enemy first. In fact in the East African campaign I have seen large forces of good soldiers routed by only a handful of men, who happened to be so fortunate as to catch the first glimpse and take advantage of it by lying in wait for the enemy to come along.

Up to this time the Settlers' Corps, the East
African Mounted Rifles and the East African Rifles,
were the only white troops in the country ; but soon
after the battle of Tanga at the coast, the Loyal
North Lancs., a fine body of regular infantry, came
to the country and took up standing camp right
alongside our lines.   Although they were strange
to our methods of warfare, they were plucky and
hardy and soon adapted themselves to local conditions.   When they first came we could not help
admiring their cheerfulness after the crushing defeat
and heavy losses at Tanga.   The stories these men
told us made some of the elder settlers' blood boil
with indignation.

We heard a great deal of Tanga from the men of
the North Lancs., who all told more or less the
same tale, although each man spoke from his own
viewpoint.   The following is the gist of a description I received first hand from a Sergeant, a short
time after the battle.

A large well-equipped force, consisting mostly of
white and Indian regulars, set out from India to
Tanga.   On arriving at the German port the troop-
ships and cruisers anchored outside the harbour and
a message was sent to the enemy to the effect that
the British meant to bombard the town ; but a
generous period was given to get the women and
children out of danger.   This prolonged grace was
the undoing of the British and resulted in the cruel
butchery in cold blood of many of our men.   The
German Commander took full advantage of every
hour.   He had only a few men at the time to defend
Tanga, but at once set his railway running day and

night at high pressure, sending almost every man in
the country who could fire a gun to Tanga, and as
an old German resident of the town said to me some
years afterwards :—

" If your side had wanted to walk into Arusha,
Moshi or any important up-country position, you
could have done so without resistance.   Everyone
was at Tanga."

Fortifications and earthworks were thrown up
and the country mapped out until the place where
our forces were about to attack was fully prepared.

When the time was up, our men landed in open
boats and barges.   The naval officers and bluejackets with their great guns were itching to bombard the place where our men were to land, thus
rendering it safe ; but not a shot was fired.

The troops were massed on the foreshore. They
started to advance towards the town and the waiting
and entrenched Germans with machine-guns opened
fire on our men, who calmly returned fire in spite
of being mown down like ripe corn.

The Germans had the position, our men were
exposed and at a disadvantage ; and with heavy
losses later slowly retired to their boats.   They were
shot to pieces and forced down to the shore ; but
the naval guns covering them now dare not fire
a shot to assist their comrades, for they did not
know how far our troops had penetrated inland
and were afraid of killing them.

The bulk of our forces embarked in the boats and
got safely away, but there were not enough vessels
to take all, as some were still away bringing equip-

ment. The poor fellows who had to remain behind desperately kept back the enemy while embarkation slowly took place, but they became weaker and weaker and at last were forced right back to the water and, seeing there was no cover, had to surrender. But the blood-thirsty enemy askaris, finding them helpless, rushed down and butchered them.

The battle is over and the venture a complete fiasco. The troops being withdrawn, the naval guns open fire and now blow the town up. The ships move off to Mombasa and the Germans collect great supplies of provisions and materials on the foreshore.

The Tanga railway again works at high pressure and the enemy troops are rushed back to their vacant posts inland.

Von Lettow's men, especially his black troops, were full of themselves at having slaughtered so many white men like sheep. The askaris' tails were now well up and a black man always fights best under these conditions, and it was a long time before we made him forget Tanga and get his tail down again.

CHAPTER VII

INTERLUDE

OUR Commander-in-Chief of the East
African Campaign had a difficult proposition before him in combating German
East Africa, for although this country was completely cut off from the Fatherland, it was self-
contained and had a huge amount of very fine
raw material from which to recruit soldiers, besides
a German Commander whose knowledge of the
country was far superior to that of any of the half-
dozen or so of our generals who were in command
at various different times. At one period it was
difficult to know who was in command on our side,
so rapidly did the Generals come and go. Some
arrived with a splash, the air full of what they would
do and had done, then gradually less and less was
heard, and then we would next hear " General
So-and-so has left and So-and-so has come to take
command."

Of course at one time we had a superior brain in
General Smuts and if he had arrived at the beginning and had been able to remain through the campaign, there would have been a very different tale.
But General Smuts had more important work to
do in other parts of the world than to stay with us
and so we lost him and again were left with a new

General. Otherwise it would have been interesting to see these two master brains really clash—his and Von Lettow's.

How the crafty old German leader, with his knowledge of the country and its intricacies, must have chuckled each time new hands took up the reins. Perhaps a little comforted, too, by the fact that thousands of miles of hostility lay between him and his own superiors, so that he was able to work out his own destiny. For here he was, though cut off, surrounded with raw material of every sort and ammunition in abundance from the ships which from time to time ran our blockade. The vast roadless spaces of almost unknown malarial and tsetse fly stricken bush assisted him to drag out his guerilla operations. It was entirely different guerilla to that of the Boer War, or in fact any other modern war, in that the vast spaces traversed were infected with this deadly fly, which prevented the use of animal draft or mounted infantry. Motor cars and lorries generally speaking were practically useless, owing to the lack of roads and the heavy rainfall. In the end we had to resort to our enemy's own method of transport, which was to carry everything on the natives' heads ; and from that time we began to have more success, though even then there was much to cope with. When there are tens of thousands of men operating on the offensive a long way from their base, you can imagine the vast number of porters which must be employed to bring up provisions and ammunition. The enemy, on the other hand, lived on the country and did all in their power to destroy food sources as they retired before our invading armies.

But I have been going too far ahead, for we are still within the year 1915 and my corps camped on the border at Manga River, some sixty miles from the foot of Kilimanjaro, doing everlasting, monotonous patrols over the scorched and waterless veldt.

War has lost some of its glamour for many of us and the men of the Settler's Corps, once so eager and keen, live for the day when they can get back to attend to their long-neglected farms. One grizzly-bearded old settler expressed the general feeling pretty clearly, I think, when he said :—

" I would not mind letting my shamba go to hell if we were only doing something ; but sitting here twiddling my thumbs while my coffee berries are falling off the trees and rotting is a little more than I can bear."

Meanwhile, as we were not strong enough as yet to invade the enemy's country and Von Lettow was too busy training his new army to invade us, we just sat down near the border. Here we stayed for many more weary months, watching, and here also later on our officers took it into their heads to turn what remained of us into proper soldiers— there were only about half the original number left.

We were given proper horses imported from India and, in place of the bandit outfit, we were dressed up in real Tommy Atkins uniform and given new saddlery. We were taught to drill and above all to salute our officers. In fact, from an unkempt rabble we were transformed into real disciplined soldiers, no doubt far more efficient and certainly smarter to look at, but at first the old hands amongst us hated it.

CHAPTER VIII

BACK TO NATURE

I THINK I personally felt the loss of freedom more than many. During the three or four years previous to joining up I suppose I had been spoilt—living a life of independence in my early youth, trusting entirely to my own resources, having cut myself off from my family at the age of sixteen, changed my name to Brown and gone out into the wilds.[1] Some may think it a good thing for a youth to be self-reliant, but it does have its disadvantages and I had to learn that independence did not work in the army. I could not at the time see the necessity of drill, hated discipline and despised the antics of my superiors, and, although none knew what restraints I made at times, I often got into the bad books of the N.C.O.'s.

When I first joined up things were very strange, and even now I had not properly adjusted myself to the new conditions. I had lived amongst the simple blacks as one in authority for several years ; now I was brought amongst my own kind as an equal, nay I was even made to feel an inferior alongside the polished and sophisticated young city men with their wit and elegance. My knowledge of natives and elephants and hunting availed but little

[1] See *From Hobo to Cannibal King*. (Stanley Paul & Co.)

here. Older men smiled if I mentioned that I had shot elephant and lion, and thought me an imaginative youngster, no doubt. As a trooper in the army I was merely one of the cogs in a wheel, to turn as the wheel was ordered to turn ; a good soldier, I was beginning to learn, is not allowed to think, but must do as he is told. Even the fighting was a poor affair to what I had imagined it would be. You were just herded along (and often by men who knew little of bushcraft) to meet an enemy similarly herded along, and then each side would fire at the other until one side gave way.

"Why could not each man be sent out into the bush-covered enemy's country with a rifle, some rations and bring back a scalp or so ? " I thought. So strong was my idea that the war could be won in this way that one day I put my views before the Sergeant-Major, suggesting that I be sent out.

" Go 'hon with you and your ideas," said he. " Better tell it to Kitchener. Here you are, if you have so much spare time, take hold of that broom and clean up the 'orse lines."

I had by this time learnt not to argue the point, and then and there I was put on to a task which lasted me some hours and certainly cured me from any more suggestions to that Sergeant-Major.

Whilst bathing in the stream flowing from the forest-clad mountain, Oldoinyo Narok, I had often looked upwards and expressed a desire to explore those heights, which nobody up to the present had done properly, although it was so near the camp. It was rumoured by Masai natives that the mountain

top was extensive and covered in tall forest, abound-
ing in elephants and rhino.   There was also said
to be a small lake up there which fed the stream
running down the mountain-side.   One or two of
the officers with a few men had gone up, more for
pleasure than on duty, but had generally turned
back on reaching the dense forest, which they
described as bristling with rhino and elephant.

On two occasions I asked my O.C. to allow me to
explore the mountain, but he would not hear
of it, saying he did not want to be responsible for
the pranks of young soldiers for whom he would
have to answer if they came to grief.   But I often
found opportunity to slip away from the noisy
camp for an hour or so, to be left alone with my
own thoughts.   One morning I determined to go
up to the forest line of the mountain.   If I started
immediately after grooming parade and got back
again for lunch, my absence probably would not
be noticed by the Sergeant-Major.

The morning was bracing and I made good headway and soon reached the old observing-post, half-
way up the mountain.   Here I stopped to rest
before continuing to climb.   The going was much
rougher now, as there was no path and after a lot
more climbing I sat down on a flat rock, this time
almost at the crest.   Here I could admire the panorama spread before me.   Directly down below could
be traced the course of the Manga stream, where it
entered a long, broad green reedy swamp, winding
away like a snake into the dry and waterless plain,
ever growing less and less, until within only some

four or five miles ceased to exist, having been
swallowed up by the thirsty earth.

The German border lay about half a mile from
the British camp, a mere imaginary line. Ten
miles away was the late enemy's post, another dark
forest topped mountain, but not so extensive as
Oldoinyo Narok and differently shaped, for up
from the top of the forest-covered crest projected a
pointed mass of rock shaped like a dog's tooth, the
peculiar feature of Longido, the scene of our earlier
fight.

At the foot of that solitary mountain, I remembered, lay some of our comrades, who would never
go back to their farms again. Some of them came
vividly before me as I looked at the panorama.
There was Tarlton, a mere boy, and others—Firley,
Billy Smith, Drake and the rest.

Turning my eyes south-east I saw some seventy
miles away the mighty Kilimanjaro rising from the
flat, waterless country. Though so far away it
looked quite near, owing to the clearness of the
morning, with its flat, extensive snow cap projecting
far above the cloud line. The morning sun shone
on the dazzling crest, which almost resembled a
white flat-topped iced cake, with the sugary substance flowing over the edge—in reality huge
mountain glaciers. Then forty miles to the right
there was a sister mountain, Meru, an extinct
volcano with one side of the lip broken away by
ancient lava flow and the other rising into a peak,
also reaching above the cloud line and covered
with snow, but not so dazzling white as that of
Kilimanjaro.

Though I had often had glimpses of the great snow mountains I had never had such an extensive and clear view ; and I looked long until with the rising sun a cloudy mantle enveloped the tops of the two distant peaks. Then I continued to climb upwards and soon came to the crest, where the formation changed from scrub and rocky boulders to dense dark primeval forest. For a time I sat down under the green foliage of the trees and then hurried back down the hill, lest I should get into trouble for being absent without leave.

I was now determined to have a day in that beautiful forest. Who knows, I might come across a tusker worth shooting up there ? So next morning I risked punishment by telling the Sergeant-Major that I had been up to the forest line and there was a great deal of wild honey in some of the big tree trunks. If I could have a day off I would fetch some down for him. I knew he was very partial to wild honey and he readily fell in with my plans, but said I must take another man with me to help carry the honey, also for safety's sake. He beckoned a trooper about my own age named New, who happened to be near, asking him if he cared to go with me to get the honey. New had just got a camera and was keen to get some photos and he readily consented, so the Sergeant-Major gave us two clean nosebags from the Q.M. Stores and told us to be gone and take care we brought the honey straight to him—also be sure the officers did not hear we were going up the mountain for the day.

We threw a few biscuits into our haversacks and left the camp by a back way and very soon were

picking our way up the rocky mountain-side.
Eventually, after about an hour of hard work, sweat
pouring from our faces, we reached the crest and
sat down to rest on the fringe of the forest. Then
we went on and came to a place where the earth
was literally covered with recent elephant spoor,
while the lower branches of the trees, undergrowth
and sapplings were trampled flat, and large
branches were torn away and stripped of their
leaves.

My companion was greatly awed and impressed.

" No wonder those officers turned back at the
forest line with creatures like these running loose.
There must be animals enough in this forest to
scare the wits out of anyone."

" I was talking to an old Masai the other day
and was inclined to laugh at his story then, but
now I am beginning to think there may be something in it after all. He told me that at this time of
year the forest on the mountain top is noted for the
number of fierce animals ; the natives say the
elephants, rhino, lions, hyenas and leopards gather
here to hold *shauris*, the chief item on the agenda
being a means of destroying their most feared
enemy—man. Just after one of these meetings the
animals are very dangerous. The elephants ramp
and tear down branches to show their strength,
the rhino ploughs up the leaf mould with his horn,
the lions roar. Should a man be near at a time
like this it would be very unhealthy for him. When
the animals part, however, they soon forget their
resolutions and man still lives on, shooting at them
with poisoned arrows, digging pitfalls at their

F

watering-places and salt licks, killing one here and another there, so that every year the animals again meet to have a fresh *shauri*. Of course the old man's story is all bunkum, although there is truth in it so far as the gathering of animals on the mountain goes."

My theory as to why the elephants and rhino come to the mountain forest at this time of the year is because the surrounding country for hundreds of miles is scorched and almost waterless, whereas the foliage up here is green and fresh and water plentiful. Herds of antelope also come in near to the mountain for the water which flows down the side, thus attracting the carnivorous animals which lurk in the foothills.

We spent hours searching for honey without success and once stumbled upon a sleeping rhino, which charged off into the undergrowth. A little further on New, who was out for blood, succeeded in killing a bushbuck which was grazing in a glade. Nearby there was a fresh spring gushing from some rocks, forming the source of a little rivulet which rippled down a timbered valley. The surroundings here were so pleasant that we determined to camp for our midday meal and filling our mess tins with water, took them up on to a rocky shelf above the spring and there kindled a fire.

After a hearty meal of biscuits and venison we must have dozed off. Hearing a floundering sound at the water just below, I looked down and was startled to see a rhino and her young drinking at the spring. Cautiously I nudged New to wakefulness and we both gazed down in silence.

After having drunk her fill the mother rhino
stepped on one side to make room for her offspring
to quench his thirst. The young one was only
about a week old and the size of a sheep, with a head
exactly like a turtle, but with a turned-up nose—
the place where the horn would one day grow.
He stepped forward most confidently, just as he
saw mother had done and sucked up a mouthful
of water, but spat it out again with an expression
which seemed to say :—

" No, you don't fool me—this is not mother's
milk ! "

He then put his forefeet in the water with the air
of a grown-up and violently pawed it, as he had
seen his elders do. His mother here became impatient with her son, pushing him out of the water
with her nose and if looks could talk, would have
been heard to say :—

" Oh, get out if you don't want to drink. You
are messing the water."

And then stepping forward she had a few more
gulps, afterwards also pawing violently with both
front and hind feet until the little pool was a puddle.
Then she lay down and wallowed in it, first on
one side then on the other. The baby all this time
was fretfully stamping about, seeming to say :—

" Mother ! Mother ! Oh, I want to wallow
too ! "

At last the old rhino came out, her whole body
black and slimy with mud, an inch thick in places,
and soon baby was wallowing to his heart's content.

At this period New, who had had the opportunity to take as many photographs as he pleased,

raised his rifle to shoot the rhino, but I stopped him just in time by pushing up the muzzle, for the horn was poor, we could not possibly make use of the dead animal and, besides, there was the baby.

After looking on a few moments longer I thought it would amuse us to tease the baby, so threw a pebble on his tummy, as the fat little legs kicked in the air. Instantly the young rhino was up and at his mother's side, looking round as much as to say :—

" You just dare to do it now and see what my mother will do to you ! "

The old rhino, sniffing danger in the air and with her baby standing close by her side, slowly turned round and round, her wicked little black eyes gleaming fire. At last she decided that the danger came from the rock ; so she glared in our direction, lunging at the air with her horn.

New threw an empty nosebag down at her and no sooner did it reach the ground than it was pierced by the sharp horn. The infuriated animal then wheeled round and round, tearing up everything nearby in the mad effort to get at the bag flopping from her horn. At last the bag came away, and making one more circle, she charged away into the depths of the forest with her baby at her heels and was seen no more.

We had not gone very much farther when I noticed a little drab coloured bird, flitting from branch to branch before us, chatting away feverishly every few seconds as if it wanted to tell us something of such importance that life and death depended upon it and there was not a minute to lose.

" Shall we follow it ? " said I.

" Follow what ? " replied New. " Surely you have not designs on catching and making a pet of a drab coloured little chatterbox of a bird like that ? If it does not shut up I shall put a bullet through it."

I smiled knowingly and said :

" That little bird, for all its plain looks, is a wiser little fellow than you think. If you had not spent so much of your time in Africa on your beloved shamba, you might have made the acquaintance of our little friend before. Just at the moment it is telling me to follow and it will take us to the most wonderful wild bees' hive ever seen, full of beautiful sweet honey."

" Oh, you are pulling my leg."

" Indeed I am not, you just follow and see."

" All right, lead on Macduff ! "

I then gave the little bird a whistle I had learnt from the Wandorobo hunters and which meant we were coming. The bird, giving a joyful little flutter, led us steadily onwards, flying from tree to tree, ever watching over its shoulder to see if we were following, ever answering my whistle with the same monotonous chatter. We had to hurry to keep pace with our nimble guide, stumbling over creepers, forcing our way through undergrowth, the sweat pouring from our brows.

" I wish that little bird of yours would go a bit slower. You might tell it to do so. Well, that has done us anyway," said New, rather gleefully as he stared down a great rocky ravine which lay between us and our feathered guide. " I thought the little fellow was a fraud and humbug all the time. A

creature which can chatter so much could not
possibly tell the truth, I am sure. Where is your
honey now ? Well, you are a softy sometimes—I
suppose you got this from some silly old native
legend ? "

I felt a little crestfallen and said :—

" I suppose the little bird can't help the ravine,
can it ? This case is merely unfortunate, but one
day I will show you when we meet another bird of
this species in better country. Meanwhile I don t
know what we can do about the Sergeant-Major s
honey—I suppose he will blow me up."

We were wending our way slowly back on our
tracks, when again the drab coloured bird settled
on a branch right before us and this time really let
herself go, chatting so expressively that even New,
I believe, felt that he was being scolded, as he said
with a shrug of his shoulders and an amused laugh :—

" And what is the little chatter-box gassing about
now ? More lies, I suppose."

" Oh, she was merely telling me that as we were
such fools as to be unable to fly over the ravine,
she will take us to another hive."

With this I replied to the bird's call and she this
time piloted us along parallel with the chasm. We
went on for a short distance and came to a well-
worn elephant track which I noticed circled round
the ravine, which came to a dead end with precipitous walls. We followed the bird and found
ourselves being deliberately led back along the
opposite side until we were again almost opposite
the place where we had turned back and soon were
going in exactly the same direction as before.

" Well, your little bird certainly seems to know where she is going, after all. If the thing were not so infernally incredible I should be almost inclined to believe you."

" Oh, please don't believe me if you don't want to, old fellow. We shall soon be there anyway and you will be pleased enough to help eat the honey."

Just then the little bird was seen to flutter its wings, then dive downwards past the trunk of a dry tree.

" There it is," said I running forward and sure enough, half-way up the tree could be seen a little hole, from which bees buzzed in and out.

" Well, if that is not deliberate perversity of nature. It is almost unbelievable ! I doubt no longer."

We smoked the bees until they were all too dazed to sting and then proceeded to cut away the hard wood, making a sufficiently large hole to remove the honey and a nosebag and mess-tin were filled with beautiful white comb ; but before leaving the spot I placed a large comb full of bee bread and fat maggot-like young bees between a cleft in the branch and as we moved off the little honey bird flitted down to claim her share of the spoil. We watched her greedily pull forth maggot after maggot, and then made tracks for home getting back to camp late in the afternoon.

CHAPTER IX

A RHINO HARD WON

ONE day we received orders to evacuate all the country around Longido and Oldoinyo Narok and move some forty miles back to Bissel, which from a General's point of view, I suppose, was the more strategical position.

As months went by more and more troops arrived from overseas and made their camp here. Amongst them were a few squadrons of Indian Lancers, mounted on Australian horses, which put our mokes to shame. I remember one day going out with a dozen of these men to show them a certain water-hole and the extent of our usual patrols in which they were now to assist us. They were all very raw to the conditions of the country and their Sub-Lieutenant, an Indian of high rank who could speak English fluently, kept on asking me questions.

All the country around Bissel was full of game, entirely new and strange to the Indian troops, and as we were riding along we suddenly came upon a rhino, standing quite still and regarding us, not fifty yards away. The Indian officer at once recognized the animal from pictures he had evidently seen and asked if we could shoot it, as

the horn had some wonderful medicinal power in
his country.

I told him he could shoot anything he came
across, for as there was a war on game laws were
not upheld, though before the war this area had
been one vast game reserve. I offered to shoot
the beast for him, but he seemed to put more trust
in some of his own men, so picked out three crack
shots, who dismounted and fired simultaneously.
I heard the thud of the bullets as they struck the
solid body, but the animal trotted quietly away.
Then some more shots were fired without effect
and still the animal trotted on. At last the whole
patrol of about twelve men fired a volley—still
no results. The animal now disappeared over the
brow of the hill, so all the men mounted and gave
chase and with their swift horses soon overtook the
rhino which lumbered steadily onwards, looking
neither to right nor left. The foremost N.C.O.
charging up on horseback, now aimed a blow at
the animal's shoulder with his lance, but it glanced
off and the man made way for the next lancer,
who was more successful, succeeding in penetrating
the thick hide, though his lance snapped off at
the head when he attempted to withdraw it. He
in turn made way with the broken shaft in his
hand, and the next man had a go. His lance also
penetrated but was wrenched from his grasp and
carried off, sticking from the animal's ribs, the shaft
soon to be shattered as it passed a tree trunk. Then
came the Sergeant, a fine swordsman, and as he
galloped by he made a violent swipe at the base of
the horn with his sword, perhaps hoping to secure

this valuable trophy without going to the trouble
of slaying the monster ; but though his aim was
true the sharp blade flew back as if striking a stone,
the impact almost wrenching the sword from the
Sergeant's hand.

The rhino now for the first time made an effort
to combat his tormentors by making a murderous
lunge with the sharp horn, but the Sergeant and
his horse were much too quick for him. Then the
officer called his men to attention and made a
fresh plan of campaign. He, it appeared, decided
that the animal must be hit in front of the head to
have any effect, so the twelve men galloped forward past the rhino and dismounting lay in ambush
for him. Nothing, however, would dissuade the
animal from the course it had taken and it came
on at the same pace as before. The men fired again
and again, but nothing seemed able to stop it and
with angry snorts it was right amongst them,
grazing a horse on the flanks with its horn and
trampling a corporal under foot. However, no
bones were broken and the men again mounted
and gave chase. The rhino still held the same
course, foolishly emerging on to an open plain.
The horsemen now had a better chance and rode
in circles around the monster and as each man
went by it he discharged his rifle into the body,
until at last, I should say from sheer weight of lead,
the animal sank to the ground.

It is almost incredible to think that any animal
could have received so many direct hits and yet be
able to go on. I should say at least fifty bullets
were fired and all by trained marksmen, regular

soldiers. Most of us settlers considered one or two shots, carefully placed, sufficient for any rhino.

As I came up the men were slashing out strips of hide with their curved-bladed swords, but the prize horn resisted all their strenuous efforts for an hour before it at last yielded.

CHAPTER X

THE LAUGHING HYENA

SOME few miles outside our camp there was a water-hole named Lemabote, and as this was one of the places the enemy would most likely first make for in case of an attack, we picketed it every night.

A low circular rough stone wall about six feet in diameter was built on some high ground overlooking the water-hole and on a moonlight night it was a wonderful sight to see animals come to drink. One night in particular, when four of us took up the position, I remember how we soon heard stealthily creeping sounds below, followed by the flop-flop of several thirsty tongues in the pool. Then all was quiet again for about an hour. At last the moon rose, round and yellow, casting a silvery light over the water and in the shadow of a tree crouched three lions, the largest having a great shaggy, almost black mane. The cat-like beasts were not apparently aware of our presence and save for the occasional twitching of the point of a tail, they were motionless, intently watching a herd of kongoni and zebra on the plain, who were nervously edging nearer and nearer with a view to quenching their burning thirst, brought on by grazing for days on nothing but sun-scorched grass. But as they were evidently suspicious their behaviour was uncertain. On one or two occasions some of the leading antelope, hoping to draw the lions, would walk boldly forward to within eighty yards of the water-hole, as if meaning to have a drink at all costs, then put down their heads, kick up their heels and dash off helter-skelter, only to return again soon and perform the same tactics. Each time the two younger maneless lions would rise to their feet ready for a charge, but seeing their leader, the old black-maned fellow, lying rigid, would settle down again.

Then a little later, emerging from the tree-covered plain, seven long streaks appeared, all set at an angle of 45 degrees. Through the herd of zebra and kongoni and wildebeest they moved, towering high above and dwarfing these animals. Forward they came without hesitation, for they were giraffe and able to hold their own in a fight with lion. The two younger giraffe got towards the middle and three bulls stood between them and the crouching lions, who with fierce rolling eyes looked on savagely, occasionally uttering low growls; but the bulls watched them cautiously, ever ready to let out swiftly with their formidable heels if attacked. The females and young with sprawling forelegs, drank their fill then moved away and waited for their protectors, who now took their turn at the pool. Then the seven long streaks moved off again until they were lost in the haze of the moonlight.

The lions still remained watchful and the herds

below looked towards the water with longing eyes.
Two rhinos came, drank at the pool, wallowed and
departed, yet the lions never moved.   A spotted
hyena ambled out of the thicket, lapped up the
water, rolling his eyes in every direction and on
seeing the lions seemed to say :—

" Ah, that is all right.   I will just wait about
here.   There will be something happening sooner
or later and I shall come in for my share."

Two little jackals could also be seen hovering
about the bushes waiting for events to happen.

The young recruits at my side, almost paralysed
with awe and fear, sat motionless and with white
faces watched the crouching lions ; but we dare not
fire for fear of arousing the slumbering camp, which
relied upon us for its safety and a shot would mean
the enemy to them.

Then the black-maned lion uttered a low
rumbling growl of disgust and contempt and flicked
the point of his tail more irritably as the spotted
hyena laughingly philandered round the pool with
his mate, uttering unearthly sounds, half-human,
half-animal, resembling the hysterical cackle of
some frenzied slum woman after having partaken
too freely at the gin shop—a cruel, heartless laugh
full of malice, hate and self-contentment.

At the dead of night, watching over a lonely
water-hole, one's imagination is liable to play tricks,
and as I listened to the ghastly sound of the hyena
I could almost distinctly hear the bragging words
coming from that throat.   Perhaps it was because
I had a natural horror of these animals above all
other beasts of the wilds, for once only a few years

back I had been almost devoured by them whilst lying helpless on the veldt.

This hyena seemed to say—" Was he not the hyena of the night, who fed on fresh meat after the lion ? " He laughed on, for he was a hyena and could afford to laugh—if he got no fresh meat he could live equally well on offal and rubbish. He looked up at us and laughed a cruel, heartless laugh, for he could see some of us were livid with fear but had to stick to our post and dare not shoot. He looked down on the thirsting buck on the plains and laughed again, for they were afraid to come to the water and moisten their parched throats. He looked up at the black-maned lion and laughed in his face, for he knew this majestic creature would shrink from touching his mangy, reeking body for fear of defiling himself and, besides, was not this " King of the Beasts " his slave, who killed fat buck for his benefit ? He looked down at the sly little jackals and laughed in contempt, for did not they have to feed after him, when mighty little was left ? He was the wizard of the wilds, for the superstitious natives threw out their dead to him, and then dare not molest him for fear of also harming their brother's spirit, which they believed to dwell within him.

Then the two loathsome animals, having laughed and drunk their full, went off to lie low until such time as the King of the Beasts had killed his prey.

The moon was now overhead and the hour was past midnight, yet the congregated antelope on the plain came no nearer. The black-maned lion, growing weary of waiting, moved forward like a shadow, his long yellow body slinking away as if by magic, but the two maneless lions crouched motionless as before. Half an hour passed then a stirring and commotion was heard amongst the waiting antelope and one of their number was laid low. The lioness and the young lion pricked up their ears and moved eagerly forward to join in the feast. The hyena and jackals arose and moved nearer to await their opportunity. The spell of the water-hole was broken as if by the spilling of the blood of a victim, and within two hours antelope and zebra arrived by the dozen and half-dozen to quench their thirsts.

But why did not the animals drink in the day-time? The reason is that during this dry spell the pool was in possession of roaming Masai and their herds of thirsty cattle.

CHAPTER XI

ON LEAVE

ABOUT this time conscription came into force in East Africa and the few young men scattered here and there in the Protectorate, who had not joined anything, came along hurriedly to swell our ranks. Amongst the last dregs from Nairobi came some queer cards, many of them city bred men, no doubt in their natural surroundings quite " lads," but some of them hopelessly out of place when they first put leg across saddle and they were often a target for the mirth and ridicule of the old hands.

One day on my way to Nairobi for a few weeks leave, a friend and I were seated in Nazereth's eating-house at Kajiado, a hurriedly constructed corrugated iron and wood building, which supplied the needs of those coming and going from Bissel camp. It figured as a starting-out place for men back from leave, for here the old hands could have their last beer and say " Farewell " to the luxuries of civilization before riding off, while the new recruit would often have a stiff double whisky and soda before mounting and thrusting himself upon the mercy of some long-suffering remount which he would have to ride some twenty-five miles to Bissel camp. If he had ridden before he was a

G   97

lucky man; if not, then he would need the double whisky and more, for he was on the brink of un-known adventures.

Our train was not leaving for some hours so we had time to kill. The eating-house and canteen were entirely deserted and we sat half-dozing on empty packing-cases, when we heard heavy footfalls and hard breathing just outside, as if somebody were staggering along. We also got the distinct odour of new leather and then a tangled mound of brand-new saddlery, water-bottles and all the paraphernalia of a mounted rifleman was deposited at the very door. This was repeated three times as two more recruits came along.

"Well, let's have one more beer each and go back for our horses," said one of the men, and as the three stood in a row sipping their drinks, my friend recognized one as a man who had sold him a pair of silk pyjamas the last time he was on leave —a great hulking young fellow from a draper's shop in Nairobi. Then there were a little sharp-faced Cockney, wearing pince-nez, probably hailing from a grocer's shop and a tubby, round, red-faced youth whom we put down as a junior clerk.

The ex-draper addressed the Goanee behind the bar :—

"Will you just keep your eye on our kit while we go along and fetch our horses? And then we will saddle up, for we have a fifty-mile gallop to Bissel before sundown."

The friend at my side came to life and nudged me, for it was obvious that they had probably never had anything to do with a horse before, except perhaps when putting on their five rupees at the Tote on the Nairobi Racecourse.

At last as the glasses were drained the three men walked off in the direction of the remount depot, and in due course returned dragging behind them two weary looking ponies and an Abyssinian mule. The draper's assistant, the largest man of the lot, we noticed had the smallest mule and tied it securely to a piece of wood projecting from the canteen, at the same time saying that he always believed in tying a horse securely while he was about it. The grocer's assistant also tied his mount, but to a light empty packing-case, the while the junior clerk simply let his reins fall loose ; but fortunately his horse, being of a quiet and sleepy nature, stood stock still looking mournfully down on the ground, bottom lip hanging very low and limp.

The grocer, a bright lad, already had his saddle on his horse's back and was just crawling underneath its belly to buckle up the girth on the other side, when the Goanee inside decided that the beer on his shelf was running low and with a harsh, rending sound opened another packing-case.

Away went the horse at full gallop, the empty packing-case dangling from the end of the lead-rope, swaying from side to side and occasionally violently bumping the terrified animal's hind-quarters. Just then there was another terrific rending sound as if the whole canteen were coming down and an ear-piercing shriek from the Goanee inside, and away went the big draper's mule, dragging some of the ramshackle shop with it, the infuriated owner waving his arms to the wind. Faster and faster grew the pace, until the two panic-stricken animals were lost in a cloud of dust as they made in the direction of the remount camp.

Amidst all this tumult the junior clerk's pony stood stock still, taking not the least notice.

Our grocer friend turned round with an injured air :—

" Well, that is what I calls a dirty trick for any horses to play a fellow ! "

The junior clerk agreed with him heartily and all three turned their attention to saddling the one remaining animal, when, to use their own words, one of them would leap upon its back and gallop after the runaways. They had it all planned out.

The draper's assistant took command of the animal's head, grasping the bit firmly and amidst instructions to his companions, would occasionally address the horse with a loud : " Woa, woa ! Steady there ! "

At last the saddle was securely fixed and tightly girthed up ; but my friend and I, unseen in the shadows of the eating-house, were literally splitting our sides with mirth, for the saddle had actually been put on back to front !

" Woa, woa ! " said the draper's assistant, tugging violently at the bit as the unfortunate animal tried to get his head back into a comfortable position. " I think this horse would be quite frisky when he gets going. Just look at him now ! I tell you what, Charlie, I'll swop him for my mule."

" No, you don't," said the junior clerk, with the air of one who knows a good thing when he has it. But there was a hitch somewhere now. The two

could get no forr'ader. The cause of the perplexity
was the crupper dangling from the saddle, a use
for which they could not find. These were issued
to the E.A.M.R. for mules and small Somali ponies.

" That goes in the mouth—I mean the part which
is round and smooth comes in between the teeth to
prevent the steel bridle from damaging the horse's
teeth."

" Do you think so ? "

" Woa, woa ! Well, do you think because an
animal is dumb, he can't feel ? "

The unfortunate beast here gave a violent tug
for freedom, but was held firm by the powerful
arms of the draper.

" All right, then we'll say the thing goes in the
mouth. It is easy for you to stand there and talk,
but the strap on the thing is too short."

" Lengthen it then, can't you ? What is the
buckle for ? "

" I have lengthened it, still it is too short. I
think it is made for a horse with a shorter neck."

" No, it is not. Look ! Mine is just the same,"
said the draper. " I think you ought to loosen up
the girth a bit, shift the saddle a bit forward and
put the thing in the horse's mouth, then draw the
saddle back in place."

" Yes, by George ! That must be how they get
a cavalry charger to arch his neck. Didn't you
ever see them on Lord Mayor's Show day in
London ? Now we are in the cavalry, you know,
we shall just have to put up with a lot of unnecessary
swank like that." The speaker, who had been
looking very hard at the saddle, suddenly exclaimed:

" I think the saddle ought to come the other way round, though. That thing goes behind the tail "

Here came an angry interruption.

" Where the hell is your corporal ? Who let a horse tied to a —— damned box go through my horse lines ? You Rookies will be the death of us all in this 'ere place ! Where is your corporal ? "

" Oh, the Corporal is coming along all right. He told us to get saddled up while he had a chat with a pal. He will be along in a minute."

The Remount Sergeant, with one contemptuous glance at the recruits, walked off muttering partly to himself and partly to the three men :

" They will squirm all right when old MacNab gets hold of them in the riding school out at Bissel. He will teach you to tie your horses to empty beer cases, he will ! "

Then our train came in and we were soon joy-fully bound for Nairobi, as times were slack on the border and we had wangled two weeks' leave.

" Nairobi is good enough for me any day," said my pal, so I left him and went to Njoro and there borrowed porters to enjoy some shooting at a little spot I knew of on the Mau, some thirty miles away from the station and at an elevation of about 9000 feet. The air up here was cool and bracing and the dense forest moist and hung with moss, all a wonderful contrast to the hot and barren plains at the front.

I soon collected a family of Wandorobo trackers, who were all eager in the anticipation of some meat. My ambition was to shoot a bongo, that rare species of giant bushbuck, which lives only in dense forest of the high altitudes, feeding upon bamboo leaves and forest herbs. Although the animal is fairly plentiful in these highlands, it is very rarely seen and most difficult to get, owing to its habit of feeding and living exclusively in the dark shadows of the forest, and in East Africa at this period the number of white men who had killed a bongo could easily be counted on one hand.

I had pitched my camp at a beautiful spring, a grassy slope falling away on one side and a lofty cedar forest arising upon the other, and having sent back the porters, I settled down to do some quiet shooting in a country quite uninhabited by human beings, with the exception perhaps of an occasional Wandorobo.

The next morning the Wandorobo trackers awakened me very early and we were first going to try and get a buffalo before the herd went back to lie up in the thick bush for the day ; but early as we had arisen, they had gone back before us, in fact before it was light. So after having an early breakfast by the side of a stream, the Wandorobo led me to the great bamboo forest which stretches for miles and miles over the rolling country, only occasionally broken by the huge trunk of some giant cedar tree, straight podocarpus or branching olive.

We had been going in dead silence through the forest for nearly an hour when suddenly above us the feathery bamboos became alive with a troop of quick-moving blue monkeys and immediately they saw us they started making for safety in the heavy forest. But swift as they were on the bamboo tops the Wandorobo were quicker below, for taking up a position just where the troop was passing above, the men shook the bamboo stalks so violently that one of the half-grown monkeys lost his footing while leaping from one to another. The young monkey, however, no sooner touched the ground than it went up another stalk like a streak of lightning and was again thirty feet above us in the bamboo tops. But it had now been cut off from the rest of the mob, who had regained safety in the trees of the forest. Each time he tried to escape the Wandorobo below shook the bamboos until he again missed his footing and fell to the ground, this time to be clubbed on the head and tucked away in one of the men's leather bags and regarded as a toothsome morsel later to be roasted over the camp fire.

We had been all this time passing through typical bongo country and often saw fairly fresh spoor, but not fresh enough to follow. At last the old Wandorobo's face brightened as we got on to some very recent spoor and for an hour I followed the old man, who glided before me as noiseless as a shadow. Then by a sudden sign, a clicking noise made by the tongue to represent the call of a bird, I knew he had seen the bongo. The hunter stood stock still, pointing with his bow, saying in a whisper only one word : " *Seragoita* " (bongo).

I strained my eyes but could see nothing except the multitude of greeny yellow stalks of the bamboos against the ruddy yellow effect formed by the sun shining through the half-discarded sheath—like wrappings just fallen or still clinging to the green

CAPTURED ENGINE (WOOD FUEL) ON TANGA RAILWAY

[p. 71

IN THEIR HURRY TO GET AWAY THEY HAD DERAILED
AN ENGINE

[p. 127.

GERMAN PRISONERS OF WAR

[p. 72.

G.H.Q. ARRIVES

[p. 72.

stalks. Then suddenly there was a terrific crashing
and a herd of five bongo bounded away to safety.

For the following week I rose every morning
before dawn, trying for the buffalo first, and when
they had retired for the day into impenetrable bush,
going after bongo, but I never came up with them
again. The buffalo, too, seemed to be going to
cover earlier and earlier. Then one day my luck
changed and in the morning I bagged an old bull
buffalo who had just remained a minute too long
cropping at the sweet grass on the forest edge.
I had decided to do no more hunting that day and
was walking towards my camp through a bamboo
forest when a Wandorobo youth who was guiding
me stopped dead and regarding some spoor on
the ground said it was fresh bongo, and we followed
it for an hour or so, when I again heard that
peculiar clicking and the youth pointed straight
ahead of him. I could see no shape resembling
an animal, but merely a reddish brown blur which
I knew must be some part of a bongo, and realizing
that in another second it might crash off without
warning, I fired with the 450 Cordite rifle which I
had used for the buffalo. There was the usual loud
crashing and breaking of bamboos and then all
was quiet again. The young Wandorobo and I
walked forward and there sure enough was blood.
The animal had been hit, but where I could not tell.
For hours we followed, twice coming up with the
wounded animal which immediately crashed away
on hearing us in the distance, until at last we had
to abandon the chase and I went home disappointed.

In the morning, however, the other two older Wandorobo hunters came to the tent saying we should again take up the spoor of the wounded animal. They brought with them a dozen or so mangy dogs, with peculiar native dog-bells tied round the middle of their bodies. Some time was spent in getting to the place where we had last seen the spoor, but on arriving there the dogs at once took up the scent and ran forward, and, led by the rattle of their bells, not a quarter of a mile away we came upon the dead bongo, partly eaten by hyenas.

I had only seen a small cow bongo before, standing not much higher than a fair-sized donkey, so was not prepared for this monster, which was a bull and as large as a steer. He had a great thick pair of ivory tipped horns rising upwards with a slight screw, shaped exactly like those of a bush-buck, but very much longer and as thick as a man's arm at the base.

On the whole the animal has a very striking and handsome appearance, with its sleek, reddish brown coat covered with white stripes. Down the centre of the back, commencing from the head and running right to the root of the tail, grows a short stubbly dark brown mane—or 'ridge' would describe it better—like that of a horse which has been hogged and then neglected for a fortnight. From this at short and sometimes irregular intervals run the gay white stripes straight down the flanks, neck and rump ; but unlike the stripes of a zebra, they are straight and at a little distance the effect exactly resembles the stalks of the bamboos among which the animal has lived for many centuries. No doubt Nature gave this protection which is most effective, for I think a bongo standing in a bamboo forest is one of the most difficult things to see. Even the horns seem to resemble bamboos and those parts of the animal which are not striped, such as the head, are blotched with brown and white, splashed in such an irregular way as to entirely break up the outline and blur it into the natural surroundings.

CHAPTER XII

WILSON'S SCOUTS

I ALWAYS had an ambition to be an army scout and I often looked with envious eyes upon our ten scouts, attached to the E.A.M.R. under Captain Wilson. They rode the finest horses in the country, and a trooper in the scouts drew as much pay as a Sergeant-Major in our lot and never did a share of camp pickets at night. Their only duties seemed to be going out on mysterious reconnoitring patrols in the enemy's country, or swaggering about on their big horses.

Not long after I rejoined my squadron at Bissel I heard there were two vacancies in the Scouts and, if I applied for one, I might be accepted. So the next day, trembling with excitement, I went to the scout lines and made a personal application to Captain Wilson. After answering several questions I was told that the matter would be given consideration and you can imagine my excitement when a day later my application was accepted But the next difficulty was to get permission from my C.O. for the transfer. I had recently been promoted to Lance-Corporal and was promised to be very soon made a Corporal if I stayed. It was a great wrench to leave my old squadron and friends, but the temptation of becoming a scout was too great, so I did not let the matter rest until I got the transfer.

About a month after this all the forces at Bissel again moved forward to our old stronghold, Longido, and we scouts often crossed the fifty miles of No-man's-land to the enemy's outposts, gathering information and reconnoitring water-holes, for there was soon to be a great push forward.

On one of these occasions, under cover of the darkness, we had got right into the bed of the Ngare Nyuki River, near an enemy's outpost situated on the top of a kopje known as Ngasari. As the light of dawn came on I was sent up a tall tree to keep watch while the others watered their thirsty horses below. While the animals were drinking I suddenly noticed German mounted men coming towards us. I called down a warning and all the men below hastily prepared to flee. As I reached the ground I mounted the river bank with the Captain and pointed out to him the direction in which I had seen the enemy. Hardly had I done this when we saw the foremost Germans coming along not fifty yards away, evidently quite unsuspectingly. The Captain at once gave the word to retire, as we were only a small body, and hurrying back to the other men I took over my horse, to find someone had removed the bit when watering him and in the excitement of the alarm had forgotten to put it back, so I was left struggling with an excited, bridleless horse while all the others, who did not notice my trouble, went off at full gallop to safety. The Germans were now not more than twenty yards away and at any moment I should be exposed to their full view when they came out on the banks of the stream.

My first impulse was to mount the horse and trust to its following its companions ; but then on second thoughts I remembered the animal was still very thirsty, as it had been disturbed at its drink and would just as likely go back to the water as follow the others, who by this time were out of sight amongst the bushes.   No, I must just get the bit into its mouth first.   Although this took only some ten seconds it felt like hours, as all the time I expected to receive a bullet in the back.   When everything was ready I gave one glance behind and saw the foremost German had just emerged from the trees on the stream bank, not fifteen yards away.   He was so taken aback at seeing one of the enemy so near that a second or two elapsed before he decided to dismount and fire.   By this time, however, I had vaulted into the saddle, pressed home my spurs and in two bounds the horse carried me in between two bushes out of sight.   I followed the other scouts ; but to get free of the place, which was partly surrounded by swamp, they had to come out of the bush and cross a long stretch of open grass land which was in full view of the German outpost.   They had got half-way across before the Germans saw them and opened fire, but when I came along over the same ground a minute later the enemy were ready for me and let me have such a volley that bullets seemed to hiss and spit all around, whilst all I could do in retaliation was to sit tight in the saddle and trust to luck.   Fortunately the distance was a long one for accurate fire.   In no time I had covered half a mile and gave a sigh of relief, for I felt I would soon be out of range, when suddenly my horse gave way under me and came down on to his knees, nearly throwing me over his head. But the faithful animal regained his footing and although I could see blood running from the side of his head and expected him to collapse underneath me at any moment, he kept on and we were soon safely out of range.

Then I caught up with the others and when we halted, on examining my horse we found the wound very slight, but being just under the eye he must have fallen from the concussion of the bullet. Fortunately nobody was hit and our Sergeant attributed this good luck to the speed we were able to travel with our fine horses, many of them imported for racing before the war by well-known local sportsmen.

Our officer was greatly worried, for two men whom he had sent up on foot to scout the kopje had not returned and we feared the Germans had got them ; but soon we saw too figures coming along through the trees. They had had a narrow escape, however, and at one time were in hiding only a few yards from the enemy, but at last found an opportunity to slink away unnoticed amongst the trees and bushes.

A week or so later Wilson's Scouts had been increased by two more members, two Australians named Arnold Wienholt and his friend, Lewis. Wienholt had tried to join the overseas forces for France at the outbreak of war, but had been rejected on account of his right arm, which had been crushed by a lion on a hunting expedition in Angola, so he went back to S.W. Africa and served in the Intelligence there.   When the Germans were all cleared up in that quarter, he came on to East Africa, bringing along with him three horses bred on his ranches in Queensland.

I mention these two men for I was to see a lot of active service with them later.

CHAPTER XIII

THE BIG PUSH

IT was now over two years since the war had started and German South-West Africa had been conquered by South African troops, which released large forces from those parts. In February, 1916, General Smuts took charge of operations. Troops had been pouring in from the coast by every train and at last on March 8th, 1916, the day came for which we had been waiting so long.

The plan was to attack the town of Moshi, the terminus of the Tanga line, from two different bases. Moshi lay at the foot of Kilimanjaro. General Smuts with the largest force would advance from Taveta, then on through a gap of the Pare Mountains. Our forces at Longido would advance along the west foothills of Kilimanjaro, then on to Moshi and thus the Germans would be entrapped by simultaneous attacks from two sides.

The work of the scouts now commenced in earnest, for we had to guide the troops over the country we had been reconnoitring. The first enemy outpost about the Ngare Nyuki River put up no resistance and our mountain battery placed their guns on the top of the German fortress. One of our columns camped here while we scouts went

on half a day's march ahead, until we reached
the foothills of Kilimanjaro, which were held by
the Germans. Hiding in a kopje we watched the
enemy moving about. At last, towards midday,
we saw our main forces, under General Stewart,
approaching over the plains and our C.O. sent
word back informing him of the enemy's presence.
The infantry in extended order marched slowly but
steadily up to the Germans, who were waiting for
them. From our position, where the movements of
the troops on both sides were visible, it was like
looking at a game of chess on a huge scale.

When at last our forces were in range, the
Germans fired only one volley and fled for the forest-
clad slopes of Kilimanjaro. Then our men, weary
from long marching, camped at a stream and rested
for the day. We also joined the column later, four
of us being sent out to do more reconnoitring. We
found a large, smouldering German camp just
inside the fringe of the forest, all the enemy having
fled along a rugged path which was a short cut to
Moshi. Our column could not follow them along
this, however, owing to the artillery and heavy
transport, so we had to find a new road on the more
level country below.

As the infantry and wagons moved much more
slowly they were sent on ahead the next day and
we scouts went along to guide them. Travelling
half the day we struck a German path with telephone wire running along the side and following
this we camped at a spring called Maji ya Chai,
because the water, owing to some mineral effect, was
the colour of strong tea, yet fairly passable to drink.

The afternoon wore on, yet the cavalry and E.A.M.R. left behind did not turn up. Another trooper and myself were sent back to find and guide to camp two companies of Indian infantry, who were said to have taken the wrong path. These we found and brought into camp safely, but although we had been a long way back we saw nothing of the cavalry and E.A.M.R. Later we found that the mounted men had been engaged by a party of Germans on their way from Arusha to Moshi, who had cut in between us and them, and a sharp but short fight had ensued. However, the Germans' only concern was to get to Moshi and they went on ; but for some unknown reason the cavalry and E.A.M.R. did not proceed on their journey, causing great anxiety and confusion to General Stewart in front, who could not think what had happened to his cavalry, and had to hold up the entire advance for them, just at the period when time was so precious.

That night my friend and I on regaining camp safely with the Indian infantry were on the point of collapse, having been in the saddle or on the watch all that day and the whole night previously and we felt we could not go on like this much longer. However, we felt much better the next morning and were able to accompany our O.C. in scouting for the infantry right up to the Sonja River, at a place on the German main road from Arusha to Moshi. There was a force of enemy camped a little beyond, but they fled without firing a shot on seeing us in the distance, and we scouts now having no enemy to worry about, turned our attention to our own needs and were lucky enough to round up half a dozen chickens, which we chased round and round the wayside hotel and they were very acceptable too, as we had been marching on half rations for several days. We were just stowing the birds away in haversacks and nosebags when the advance guard of the infantry came up and hungrily gave chase to a long-legged cockerel which had proved too fleet of foot for us, but the infantry soon got him, bringing into practice some of their flanking movements.

When the mounted men eventually came up we were again attached to our old corps, the E.A.M.R., and together with the Indian cavalry we pushed forward, leaving the infantry behind this time. Finding all bridges on the main road blown up we made fresh roads for ourselves lower down, where the gorges formed by the mountain streams were not so deep, and after a series of forced marches we reached the Tanga railway line at a point southeast of Moshi. This we cut, but unfortunately the last train had already passed on to Kahe. Meanwhile, by another route, our infantry under General Stewart had pushed on to Moshi, linking up with General Smuts' forces which, after fighting fierce battles around Latema, Reata and Himo, had at last driven the Germans from the heights and advanced through the gap formed by the Pare Mountains and the south-eastern foothills of Kilimanjaro and so Moshi was now in British hands.

Von Lettow, the German General, retired to a prepared position at Kahe, and we, Wilson's

Scouts, joined General Sheppard's brigade just in time for the heavy engagement there. The fighting started in the afternoon and got hotter and hotter as night came on. All that night through the bright moonlight the battle raged ; the enemy, with great cheering and war-like blasts from their bugles, repeatedly charged the Indian infantry, who remained as firm as a rock. Taking cover in their hastily dug rifle pits, they mowed down the enemy as they came up and in the morning dead lay within ten yards of the British lines.

On the following day there was more heavy fighting and then Von Lettow retired to Lembeni, twenty miles away, leaving behind at Kahe an abandoned 4.1 Konigsburg naval gun, mounted on a cement floor, and having also expended far more rifle and machine-gun ammunition than he could afford. However, the enemy's luck held, for just at this time their second ship ran the blockade of our navy and brought to the German troops ammunition, as well as machine-guns, howitzers, clothing and even foodstuffs. So they were still as well off in equipment as we were.

CHAPTER XIV

SCOUTING ALONG THE PANGANI RIVER

THE rainy season had now set in and operations ceased for some months. As the Germans had fled from Arusha, a very healthy place, the E.A.M.R. with other mounted men were sent there to escape the deadly tsetse fly, which infected the area about Kahe. Near Arusha we remained in a standing camp for a time and it was pitiable to see our beautiful horses every day succumb one by one to horse sickness.

Our camp was situated right at the foot of the forest-clad Mt. Meru, an extinct volcano rising 15,000 feet above the sea level and with a snow cap on the top which fed numerous streams of water, as clear as crystal, running down the side from the melted snow. One of these passed alongside our camp, only a few miles farther on to be swallowed up and parched as usual by the endless dry bush country. All the country around this beautiful mountain was composed of volcanic ash, therefore exceedingly fertile and very thickly populated by a native tribe, the Warusha, who understood irrigation and made full use of the many streams flowing from the snow, leading them off in cunningly engineered channels on to their crops of maize and groves of bananas. Indeed, we had come to a land of plenty, where in addition to our rations we could buy for a few cents great bunches of ripe bananas and vegetables of every kind in abundance.

As we had nothing to do, a pal and I amused ourselves by robbing honey barrels made out of sections of hollowed trunks and suspended high up in the branches of gigantic trees. One of us would climb the tree and with a rope gently let the barrel down to earth, where the other would be ready to receive it with a smouldering fire, to smoke the bees until they were so dazed that we could remove the honey with a minimum of stings. The natives reported their losses to the O.C. troops, but we went about the robberies so cunningly that we were not found out, until one sad day a honey barrel fell from the tree and was immediately cracked and split in several places and out of the gaps came bees like a cloud. My pal went off roaring with pain and the bees after him. Then they discovered me up the tree and began to sting me in every quarter. There was no time to climb down the tree, so I leapt about twenty feet to earth, being almost stunned by the impact, and hastily made off in the direction of the stream. When the angry bees at last passed on, there was not an inch on my body which seemed comfortable. For some time I continued to lie in the reeking, muddy pool. Then I went to look for my pal and in spite of all our troubles I could not help smiling, for his face was swollen beyond all recognition, resembling a plum pudding, or some over-fed baby which could not see out of its eyes for rolls of fat.

Our troubles were by no means over, however,

for we had to return to camp sometime, when it would be obvious who had been stealing the natives' honey. But, fortunately for us, we had shared some of the spoil of more successful days with the Sergeant-Major, who now allowed us to lie up in a tent until we could face the world again. After this we lost all interest in bees and whenever we saw a honey barrel in a tree we gave it a wide berth, remembering our C.O.'s orders not to interfere with the natives' property !

Time hung very heavily, but occasionally one or two of us were able to get away for a ramble, when we would go up into the cool forest growing on the slopes of the mountain and spend the time exploring the gorges and ravines, and if sufficiently far away from camp, shooting monkeys with our service rifles.

At last we got our marching orders and went back again to Moshi via Kajiado and Voi, as the more direct route was reported to be an endless quagmire, churned up by the numerous transport vehicles. After camping for a while at M'buyuni we started on the great march down the Pangani River, all the time running parallel with the Tanga railway. The country for the first part was entirely uninhabited and in many places a road had to be hewn out through the bush. I was included amongst picked scouts directing a large gang of natives with matchets and a powerful army searchlight mounted on an ox wagon ; from 8 p.m. until dawn we cut a path through the bush, which was never before traversed by man. At dawn the native labourers were completely exhausted and dropped

down by the roadside to sleep, which was not
surprising as they had also been marching and
carrying heavy loads all the previous day ; but the
thick belt of bush was now pierced and the army
marched on through more open country.

At midday we turned in towards the beautiful
even flowing river and camped on the banks, and
those of us who had been up all night slept like
logs. I, personally, was almost too tired to eat,
but others threw out hook and line and hauled in
great long, wriggling, scaleless mud fish, which
though repulsive to look at, were excellent eating.
The Pangani River was also simply swarming with
crocodiles, several of which could be seen dozing
on the far bank. These huge reptiles lived on the
mud fish and occasionally pulled in antelope and
even buffalo as they came to drink. As I closed
my eyes, lying safe on the high bank shaded with
green foliage, the last thing I saw was one of these
reptiles also sleeping peacefully in the mud and
reeds below. How I envied that creature, who
could sleep on and on by the clear flowing water
undisturbed, while we were only able to snatch a
wink here and there as opportunity allowed. I
hardly seemed to have slept a minute when the
Corporal was again rousing us, for we had to do
some more scouting. Some of the men were already
saddled, so I hurriedly threw on my saddle and we
all cantered forward.

The trees were very much thinner and we made
good headway, soon passing the advance guard and
then making towards the railway, which was ten
miles off. When about five miles from it we

travelled parallel with the line for a long way, but
never a living being did we see, except a few oryx
and smaller antelope. The country in these parts
seemed entirely devoid of human life, nothing but
endless bush and the great broad river of clear cool
water flowing onwards. Again we camped at the
river side, then marched on once more. The
country became more mountainous now and a
long range of hills ran parallel with the river. Here
could occasionally be seen a native village nestling
right down by the river, yet never any signs of the
enemy, although we well knew they were along the
railway a few miles off, evidently too busy retiring
to their prepared position to worry us. The next
day we were sent forward with two squadrons of
Indian cavalry, who were doing the advance guard
for the column and after several hours ride we
sighted a kopje in the distance and noticed it was
occupied by the enemy ; but it only turned out to
be an outpost and they fled without firing, as the
cavalry charged and took the kopje.

We now were coming to a great bottle neck,
formed by the river on one side and the continua-
tion of the Pare range of mountains on the other,
while the railway ran between the two. Narrower
and narrower grew the bottle neck, and across this
space the Germans had made their earthworks,
meaning to make a stand at last, for here they
could not be outflanked and we were bound to
attack them from the front. Our work as scouts
was now temporarily done ; soon the infantry would
be along, so to avoid the snipers we retired into some
bushes and hid our horses and before long a bloody

battle raged. Then we got orders to scout the enemy's left flank and ascertain how far it extended up the mountain, so we returned for half a mile or so and then cut across the German railway. As we did this a few shells burst amongst us, but we put spur to the horses and soon were across the railway clearing, out of sight amongst the trees and on the other side of the line. The bushes, cacti and undergrowth were very thick on the foothills and in some places we had to dismount and lead our horses while we chopped out a path.

At last we arrived at a place fairly high up and overlooking the ground on which the battle was raging, only some three-quarters of a mile away. We hid our horses in a hollow and the Captain with four of us climbed a little higher up and watched proceedings below. We could see for miles and miles on every side over country covered in thick bush. Away in the distance rose a great cloud of dust stretching a long way back, which was our transport coming on.

Boom ! Roared a German 4.1 naval gun, fired from a railway truck below us, and then, as we looked ahead, right amongst our transport eight miles away rose a great cloud of dust from the explosion. Again and again the gun fired, but we had nothing to touch it for range, and each time with sickening hearts did we see that explosion land right in our columns. It was the first time I had seen a big gun at work, and as it was right under our noses and firing at our own side the accuracy and power of the explosions seemed all the more diabolical. Every time a shell exploded a huge cloud seemed almost to envelop the whole column, and I had the vision of dozens of transport wagons and scores of fine soldiers being blown into the air with each shot. But still it continued firing, and the long cloud of dust formed by the transport came on nearer and nearer, as if nothing unusual were happening.

I mentioned my feelings to a trooper at my side, suggesting that hundreds of the poor devils must be blown up already, but our Captain who had naval experience said :—

" For all the noise that gun and its shells are making I don't suppose it kills half a dozen men with every second shot, because I think they are only firing armour-piercing shells which they got off the cruiser *Konigsburg*."

And he was right ; for, as we afterwards heard, the casualties were comparatively very light, in spite of the deadly accurate shooting.

The sun went down leaving behind it a vivid glow of every shade imaginable in the cloud banks lying along the distant eastern horizon. Flocks of wild geese came flying in from the river and swamps, to spend a peaceful night on the crags above us, but hearing the commotion soared fearfully away. The hot wind dropped and the normally peaceful hour of gathering darkness was shattered by the erratic, stuttering rattle of the machine-guns below and that loud, harsh booming of the naval gun, which now, as dusk came on, spat a great streak of fire at every shot.

We crouched there in our hiding-place as if spellbound, watching for the great spurt of flame

rising from the gun below, then the explosion miles
away amongst our transport, until darkness came
on and the battle simmered down as if in slumber.
We knew in reality, however, that down there in
that apparently peaceful hollow were men both
black and white, glaring at each other's lines, ever
on the alert for the slightest move and still more
bloodshed and murder ; the German askaris lying
well sheltered in their prepared rifle pits and
trenches, while our men would be taking advantage
of every moment of the lull to dig themselves in,
their faces grimy with long days' travelling over
dusty roads and drawn with hunger ; their eyes
bloodshot from forced marching and want of sleep,
but ever watching while they dug away at the hard
unyielding earth. Around them would be lying
many of their comrades who had passed on and
would need to do no more thirsty marches in baking
Africa.

We stayed all night up on the slopes of the mountain, our horses and ourselves parched with thirst as
the water was out of reach, but we dared not move
—our little party of ten must keep watch for any
unusual flanking movements.

Early the next morning, three men including
myself were sent on to two other rocky and bush
covered spurs, forming the foothills. We left our
horses behind and crept forward from boulder to
boulder and bush to bush. When we reached the
ridge we saw the Germans quite near, advancing
towards us, extended over half a mile of ground.
They were no doubt preparing for a flanking movement and as they started climbing we stealthily

retired back to our Captain, reporting what we had seen. Later we received news that the Rhodesian Regiment and others had rushed the enemy and driven them out of their position and so they were forced to withdraw their flanks.

We then went down to the Pangani River, which flowed onwards, taking no heed of the quarrels of men above, but none the less willing to quench their thirsts and moisten the parched throats of any who came to its banks, and we and our horses drank as we had never done before.

The Germans had a cunningly prepared position of defence in this bottle neck, which besides having the other advantages described had the railway convenient to move heavy artillery and bring up stores and reinforcements and eventually to quickly retire by. To further strengthen the position they were building a most elaborate bridge of sawn timber for retreat across the river, should they be forced that way ; but our rapid advance had compelled them to retire by rail before the work was completed. In their hurry to get away they had derailed an engine and several trucks, which we found lying by the rail side.

CHAPTER XV

TRANSFER TO THE INTELLIGENCE DEPARTMENT

THE next advance was to Buiko, a beautiful little town nestling by the banks of the Pangani, the railway station of which the Germans were doing their best to blow up and destroy when we came along and drove them onwards, and there were packets of undischarged dynamite all ready with detonators and fuses, in all sorts of places, which the enemy at the last moment forgot to light up.

At Buiko we rested for a day and I shall always remember this place, for another scout and I came upon a large iron safe, standing about five feet high and too heavy to move. As it was securely locked, we were sure it was full of gold or some other treasures and if we could only open it our fortunes would be made. So for two hours we tried to force the lock, but the infernal thing was so strong that we could make not the slightest impression upon it, and we broke the points of bayonets and other implements of war, without the slightest success. We were determined to get the door open somehow, though, and I was in the act of bringing undischarged dynamite charges from the partly destroyed railway water tower, when alas our hopes were dashed to the ground. For along came our Corporal saying we were to saddle up with all haste and ascertain whether a large bridge, reported by the Air Force to be across the Pangani, was a myth or not.

After a great deal of searching on the thickly vegetated banks, we found the supposed bridge to be merely a few sticks and poles used by the natives for crossing. Hardly had we got back and I was once more making towards the safe, with the dynamite in my haversack, when a messenger came hurrying to tell us we must again saddle up as our C.O., with his full complement of ten scouts, was to escort General Hoskins to M'komazi, the next station, where he wanted to have a chat with General Hannyngton.

We reported the existence of the safe before we left and later learnt that it only contained the railway books !

M'komazi was about four miles away, just around a sharp bend in the railway. Our General soon came along on horseback and unattended by any staff, rode side by side with our Captain, while two men formed an advance guard and the remaining eight of us rode behind. We travelled through some bush country and on coming to the crest of a hill found that M'komazi station was still in the hands of the enemy.

" Never mind," said the General, " we will just wait here and I expect Hannyngton's advance guard will be along presently and drive them out. He should be very near by this time."

So we lingered amongst the bush overlooking

the enemy's station, when we saw in the distance Hannyngton's brigade advancing. There was a stir and bustle amongst the enemy, who were getting ready to receive the advance guard. They were up to their old game again, which was to shoot down a few of the foremost men and then make off.

" Well, I think we shall be able to save a few lives here," said the General, who was standing on an ant heap, which owing to the dense bush was the only place from which he could see the Germans. Then he jumped down to make room and half a dozen of us scrambled up the ant hill, which was pretty small for us all, and hanging on to each other we fired off a few rounds. The range was rather a long one but our firing had the desired effect, for the Germans were so surprised to hear shots coming from this unexpected quarter that they immediately boarded some waiting push-trollies and went off at full speed.

Between Buiko and M'komazi stations the railway gave a sharp curve and as we came upon the line suddenly we disturbed more Germans and native labourers, busy making excavations for a mine to blow up a bridge ; but on our approach their pickets gave warning and they made off so quickly into the bush, that we could not get a shot.

Then crossing a stream we went on to M'komazi and without any further disturbance we met General Hannyngton's brigade, which had been for days marching almost parallel with us, many miles away on the other side of the Pare range. They said they had come in for a good share of shelling with a long range naval gun that morning

I

and the previous night, as they passed through a gap formed by the Pare and the Usambara Mountains.

Soon after this Wilson's Scouts were broken up owing to the death of many of our horses through tsetse fly and I and two or three others were transferred to the Intelligence Department as Intelligence Agents, ranking as first-class warrant officers. The work would be a great deal more interesting as each man was to have his own native askaris and N.C.O.'s under him as soon as more askaris were trained at Headquarters, and I looked forward to shortly being O.C. of my own little scouting party.

Meanwhile I was to work in conjunction with two other I.D. agents, Wienholt and Lewis, who, though otherwise keen soldiers and good scouts, knew little of the local native language or conditions.

Our first trip was to reconnoitre the country southwards towards Handeni, a place on the German trolly line connecting the Tanga and Dar-es-Salaam railways. The main objects of this trip were to see if there was sufficient water supply *en route* for a brigade to march across country, also to surprise Handeni and to find out from the natives, who were always very friendly towards the British, if there were any considerable forces of enemy lurking in these parts which might attack our column, flanks or lines of communication.

We crossed the Pangani River and marching southwards through open bush inhabited by elephants and numerous other game, came upon a friendly native village of the Wakwafi tribe. They

gave us milk and the headman of the village of
Manyata offered to supply us with guides the
next day. As night was coming on we camped in
some scrub about a quarter of a mile from the
Manyata, which is formed by a circle of rude native
hovels with a thorn tree barricade in between, so
as to also serve as an enclosure for the cattle.
We slept well until midnight, when a prowling
lioness found a stray calf, which must have been
forgotten, outside the enclosure. We took little heed
of prowling animals now, but this one, evidently
thinking that the opportunity was a splendid one
for educating her half-grown cubs, allowed them
to try their novice hands, or rather claws, at pulling
it down ; the result being that for hours we were
kept awake by the bellowing of the unfortunate
calf and the playful growls of the cubs. They
chased the calf in every direction and several times
came right by our camp, and as we always slept
without a fire at night when out scouting, it would
be quite possible for the family of frollicking lions
to run right into us before they discovered our
presence. Knowing the temper of a lioness with
cubs it was difficult for us to get any more sleep.
At last, however, the bellowing of the calf grew
weaker and weaker and nothing more could be
heard in the stillness of the starry night, save the
occasional distant wailing of a jackal. We then all
settled down to get some rest, for we still had a hard
day before us.

In the morning we went to the Manyata and asked
for the village water-hole and were told there was
none, for the Wakwafi like other Masai tribes have

no use for water, except for their stock, so place
their villages several miles from any. The cattle
graze in the direction of the water once a day to
drink, but the natives never use it for their own
toilet. When they want to appear smart they
merely rub another layer of grease and red earth
over their bodies. The women do occasionaly
wash out their milk calabashes and cooking pots,
but not with water ; their cattle in fact supply all
the necessaries of life, they drink the milk, eat the
meat and regularly tap so much blood per week
from the jugular vein of each ox, which they drink
raw or boiled. Although they live for months at
a stretch thus entirely on animal food, should
natives of other tribes bring along grain or meal
they will often barter it for living sheep or beef ;
but all the Masai tribes are much too indolent to
grow any grain themselves.

Securing two guides from the village we started
off through flat, bush-covered country in the
direction of Handeni. Once while marching along
we very nearly ran into a patrol of Germans, but
as they were only a small party like ourselves,
probably also Intelligence scouts, both sides slunk
away into the bush. After this we decided that the
smaller our party the better chance we should have
of slipping past any patrols, so Lewis with the three
pack mules and four askaris went back to await us at
a certain spot, and Wienholt, myself and the guides
travelled on for two days, until we arrived at a
place where we could see Handeni from the top
of a high tree. As we had now found out all we
wanted to, and it was necessary for us to hurry back

with the information, picking up Lewis safely we eventually came upon our own column, now moving along the right bank of the Pangani.

A little later on there was a sharp fight at Makalamo, where the Germans had again taken up an advantageous position and waited for us. When they were pushed out of this position they retired down the trolly line which ran towards the Central railway, tearing up the rails and doing as much damage as they possibly could to retard our pursuit.

A few days later the three of us were again sent out with the same four askaris and Wakwafi guides, this time on a trip which would take us at least three weeks. The object of the trip was to scout the country in the direction of Kiberachi, a place about fifty miles away in country still held by the enemy. Our column at this time was living from hand to mouth, owing to bad roads and a long line of communication. A few motor lorries just managed to keep the troops alive on a very bare half-ration, so all that we could draw for the long trip at the Quartermaster's stores was a few pounds of maize meal and a little sugar and a spoonful or two of coffee. Yet we had to live somehow. We might be able to exist by killing game or getting something from friendly tribes, but the thing which would hit us hardest was being short of tea or coffee, for these could not possibly be obtained from the natives, and the water in these parts, away from the Pangani, was often a thick, stagnant greenish liquid, smelling most abominably.

So we began our journey a little down-hearted, for we had not been able to have the good feed we

generally indulged in when getting back to Headquarters after a long trip.

On consulting the guide we found the best way
to make the start would be to move back about
four miles along the column's line of communication and then strike southwards, by the sandy bed
of a dry watercourse which cut a way through a
patch of otherwise almost impenetrable thorn bush.
We had just about reached this place when Wienholt sighted a motor lorry ploughing along the
deeply rutted road. He ran forward into the road
holding up his hand, and when he had brought
the ponderous vehicle to a standstill went and
chatted to the driver. We did not hear what he
said, but Lewis and I standing at a distance had
our suspicions that a tip changed hands, for immediately, quite against Army regulations, bags
were opened and our mate came back with coffee,
tea and brown sugar, sufficient to last us for the
entire trip. With these luxuries we could keep
going quite comfortably by getting food from the
native tribes, who would probably gladly feed us
if they had the food to spare. If not, we would just
have to take it by force, for information was
required for the Army and live we must. With
so many enemy about it would be out of the question to shoot game, for to fire a shot would
immediately give our position away.

For a whole day we travelled up the dry bed
which in the rainy season was a swift-flowing
tributary of the Pangani. We emerged on some
open country and the following day while marching
along, Wienholt contracted malarial fever, but

although shaking with ague he kept bravely on. That evening we came to a pan of dirty water on which swam two wild duck and with a small ·22 Remington repeating rifle, which made very little report, I bagged one of the birds and soon had some broth boiling for Wienholt. The next morning he was a little better and we all marched on again. In chatting with some of the Wakwafi I heard rumours of bloodshed and raids between them and Masai, who were taking advantage of the fact that the German administration were too occupied with other troubles to give proper heed to their doings. One day on a lonely path we came upon a most blood-thirsty looking crew of some fifty Wakwafi armed with muzzle-loader flint-lock guns, spears, buffalo-hide shields and murderous looking knives and clubs. They were acquainted with our guides and told us they were on the way to punish some Masai who had murdered a youth herding some cattle and tried to drive off his herd, though, it seemed to us from their general appearance that we had more probably caught them on their way to surprise and rob the inmates of some unsuspecting village. But these things did not affect us and we had our own axe to grind, so we left them and went on our way.

A few days later we heard we were fairly near Kiberachi and rumours of Germans were about, but we must go on if we wanted to make a true report of the forces in this district and its neighbourhood.

For a week we had all been drinking putrid green water and were feeling pretty bad, but this morning Lewis became so ill with fever that we had to leave

him behind with one askari. Wienholt and I had
not gone half a mile farther when our three remaining askaris said they also were ill and wanted to
stay behind with Lewis. I examined them carefully and found they had no temperature whatever,
the trouble being that the four askaris we had been
given were untrained cast-offs from two other
Intelligence agents, who would naturally not give
up their best men ; for unfortunately many of our
early I. D. askaris lacked the strict training and
discipline which is so essential to a black soldier.
To make matters worse they had just been talking
to the guides who had evidently told them that there
was a large force of Germans in the immediate
neighbourhood and that our own nearest forces
were over fifty miles away, so they were suffering
from nothing but sheer funk. One man even
dropped his rifle and bolted back, when he came
very near to being shot by Weinholt.

Both of us were suffering from a low fever and in
a pretty bad temper and in no mood for argument,
so we gave the three askaris to understand that the
first man who hesitated again would be shot down
on the spot. They could see we meant it and went
forward sullenly with no further words.

Our Wakwafi, however, were quite willing to go
with us, although if they were caught they would
be shot for spies and traitors.

Owing to the number of German pickets and
patrols we marched during the night, by dawn
hiding on a hill overlooking the large enemy camp
near Kiberachi, but as it got light we could see the
last of the Germans' rear guard marching out of

. . . DID ALL IN THEIR POWER TO DESTROY FOOD
SOURCES AS THEY RETIRED . . . WATERING
TANKS . . .

[p. 73

E.A.M.R. GYMKHANA AT BISSEL, TUG-O'-WAR

E.A.M.R. GYMKHANA AT BISSEL, TENT PEGGING

[p. 108.

the camp. We first thought they were leaving the place for good to reinforce their comrades, who were now engaging our troops about Handeni, but soon we learned from some of the local natives that they were only shifting camp a short distance—we could even see the smoke from the fires of the new camp amongst some rolling country.

Feeling sure the friendly natives would warn us of approaching danger, we went right down into the German camp and amongst the several large grass buildings we found two crowded with living skeletons—poor unfortunate blacks who could barely move from weakness due to over-work and dysentery. Now the Germans, hearing our columns were advancing, had left them behind without medical attention, to take their chance until the British arrived. The unfortunate natives had not even anyone to bury their dead or collect and cook their food—a patch of hard dry maize, hanging from the stems in an adjacent field. Most of the sick had no blankets to protect them from the cold, damp night air and some of their naked bodies lay still in death while masses of them lay huddled together outside, trying to get some warmth from the morning sun. Others, a little more energetic, crawled feebly towards the maize field and chewed at the hard raw grain, the worst diet for a dysentery case. These natives—in the German's eyes—were only beasts of burden. They had done their work and now were cast aside to perish, unless the English took pity on them.

The sight of so many naked moving skeletons gave us the creeps and we turned our backs and

moved off, the sickly smell of the place haunt-
ing us.

The Germans, although they treated our wounded
and prisoners with terrible brutality in the early
part of the war when they were sure the Fatherland
would be victorious, were still so confident of
British humanity that they now made a habit of
leaving behind them their sick porters, even their
own women and children, as at Wilhelmstal and
Arusha, finding it cheaper and more convenient
that we should feed them, while they fought
unhampered. I often wonder what would have
been the fate of any white women and children
we might have left behind, should the tables have
been turned and had they been the invaders instead
of us. The Germans, however, took good care not
to leave behind any sick askaris ; these were given
careful medical attention and every consideration.

We had now achieved our object in locating the
enemy and had also obtained a great deal of valuable
information which we must take back to headquarters, so we turned to make our way to our
own column, which had, we heard from friendly
natives, moved onwards beyond Handeni.

First we went back one day's march on our
tracks to pick up Lewis in his hiding place. With
the aid of local natives we passed several more
German pickets and travelled through country
thickly populated by a very industrious and intelli-
gent tribe somewhat resembling the Swahilis, who
readily gave us food and supplied us with guides.
Here, much to our surprise, quite an ordinary
looking native, dressed in his native garb, came up

to us grinning from ear to ear with pleasure and addressed us in fluent English. It appeared that in his young days the man had joined a British steamer at Dar-es-Salaam and for ten years was away from his country, serving as stoker or deck hand, and visiting nearly all the ports of the world.

Wienholt, who could not speak Swahili, had always expressed a great desire to be able to hear the opinions of a native first-hand and felt that here was a mine of information ready to be tapped, so metaphorically speaking, he fell upon the man's neck, plying him with innumerable questions. When I came back from a visit to a village some hours later, I said :—

" Well, I suppose you are a great deal wiser now ? "

But I could see he was not at all satisfied—something had gone wrong. The trouble was that although the man was only too eager to be communicative, he had after all only a native's mentality and knew very little of present happenings beyond his own village circle. Also, the African can be a most dull creature if questioned on blunt Western lines, but most enlightening if gradually drawn out of his shell and allowed to explain things in his own way.

We eventually came upon a fine German rubber estate at a place called Kwedi Boma. In the midst of the plantation stood a magnificent double-storied dwelling-house. The Germans had only evacuated it the previous day and had left it in charge of a miserable-looking Goanee, whom we arrested, as the natives told us he had caused large trees to be felled across the road in order to retard the British advance.

We entered the large house and helped ourselves to whatever we fancied. The farmyard was full of chickens and ducks, which were very welcome, as we were starving and our men soon had a dozen or so of the birds rounded up and their necks wrung. One of the most valuable finds in the house was a bottle of quinine, for all three of us had had fever on us for the past week, but dare not give in though we were wretched enough and had run through our small supplies of this valuable drug. Owing to the nature of the bush country and the night marching we were reduced almost to rags and on examining the German's wardrobe upstairs Wienholt's eyes caught sight of a pair of khaki drill trousers. Immediately he secured them as his prize, for his own trousers were out at the knees, in fact " letting in light and air in every quarter," as he expressed it.

But when he came to put the new pair on he found much to his disgust that the previous owner, a Herr Toutloff, was very corpulent, for the garment hung loosely about his legs, while the waist was big enough for two men.

I said, looking on with interest :—

" You will have to give the things away to the boy. You can't possibly wear those."

But Wienholt was not to be put off so easily—he folded the extra cloth back and buckled on his belt.

Lewis and I were most grateful to Mrs. Toutloff and Miss Toutloff, who supplied us with ample pairs of socks, or, rather, they were stockings before we cut them down. Our own socks had long since ceased to exist, for it was as much as the army transport could do at this period to keep the troops supplied in food, new issues of clothes being quite out of the question.

The following day we struck country which had already come under the influence of our invading armies, so as there was little danger of running into the Germans we took to the open road and as the three of us marched along chatting merrily together on trivial matters. It was a great relief to talk freely again and above a whisper. The quinine had also done us a lot of good and both Wienholt and I were almost ourselves again, although poor Lewis was still pretty bad.

Wienholt was particularly cheerful and caused me great amusement by his clever imitation of old Herr Toutloff. None of us had seen him in the flesh, though we were fairly well acquainted with his dimensions. Anyway Wienholt, who could speak German, gave us the most lively impersonation of an old Hun complaining to a German General with great concern that one of the three *schwiner Englander* prisoners (meaning ourselves) had been found wearing his trousers. The threats rained upon us were terrible to hear and the German General shaking his head sadly had to admit that we were very, very wicked *schwiner Englander* indeed and would truly have to be severely dealt with. Then to old Toutloff's great horror and our great concern, as we were trying to hide our ankles, the fat German finds that we are all three wearing his wife's and daughter's stockings ! At this all the Germans are too horror-stricken for words.

So much for this clever bit of play-acting which helped to shorten a long day's march, but poor old Wienholt little knew that within only a few weeks he would in reality be a prisoner of war, caught wearing those very trousers and no doubt Mrs. Toutloff's converted stockings, too.

As we drew near to Handeni we sent a message to General Headquarters, saying that we were coming in and asking for a stretcher and medicine to be sent out for Lewis. The next day General Hannyngton himself drove out in his car to meet us and question us about the enemy's country and took back Lewis and the Goanese prisoner.

We plodded on and the following day got back to the British line of communication, having been away for nineteen days. We had been able to exist in the enemy's country for so long a time without discovery only on account of the friendliness of the natives. Often when meeting fresh natives we would introduce our party as one sent to spy out the land for the English, whose great armies would drive out the Germans and establish justice and prosperity where little justice had been before, and our scouting and very existence was always made easy for us by these natives, though they often guided us trembling with fear of German vengeance.

We now proceeded to march on along a track through the bush, deeply rutted by wheels, and passed dead mules and horses by the roadside, even too numerous for the local vultures and hyenas to cope with. The country which the column had been marching through was infected with tsetse fly as well as horse sickness, so the poor animals very seldom managed to keep alive for more than a month at a time and fresh animals were brought forward to render their little service, in turn being infected by fly and left to rot by the roadside.

We eventually caught up to the advance column at Lukigura River, where it had been held up for a few days. Here I met familiar faces of our old unit, the E.A.M.R., greatly reduced in numbers now, chiefly owing to the ravages of fever and dysentery.

During our absence the column had advanced from the Tanga line along the trolly lines with much the same hardships as before—now stopping to engage the Germans, now pushing the enemy on before them. Our troops and animals suffered much from the scarcity and badness of water. About Handeni, now miles back, the Germans had left behind them again large numbers of their dying porters, as many as two hundred in one place, often wasted to the last degree from neglect and sickness. The part through which they had travelled was described by my friend in the E.A.M.R. as foul with pestilence, especially dysentery, which spreads so rapidly amongst a marching army with crude sanitary arrangements. To help spread the disease and perhaps show their *Kultur*, the Germans had caused their askaris to foul some large building, which might have been useful to shelter our wounded and sick from the blazing sun, no doubt thinking the act a huge joke against us. The man who related his experiences said the stench in these places was simply awful.

CHAPTER XVI

A TRIP THROUGH UNKNOWN COUNTRY ; TRIBAL DISTURBANCES ; LOST IN THE BUSH

THE three of us had only two days' rest when we were again summoned to General Headquarters and our C.O. on the staff gave us a rough outline of operations which were about to start in three days' time. The main column was to make a push for the Wami River seventy miles away ; we were to dodge the German advanced outposts at night, go two days' journey onward until well behind the enemy's lines, then march parallel with the advancing British army, roughly about forty miles away on its flanks. It was feared that a large force of enemy was concentrating at a certain place on the Central Railway and would march in to make a surprise attack on our flanks and cut the line of communication. Should we hear of such a force we must bring in word at once.

As we heard the words from the Staff Officer and watched him trace an imaginary line on the map, I knew that we were in for a rough time—in short were being given a pretty tall order. We should perhaps have to be behind the German lines for several weeks and, besides doing our scouting and reconnoitring work, have to forage to feed ourselves and our men as well, for there were no surplus rations in the camp to give us.

We still only had our four original askaris, but by this time we had knocked some discipline into them and, as we had now come back twice unharmed from behind the German lines, they were beginning, I could see, to have a considerable amount of respect for our methods, though we could not put any trust in them for obtaining information and generally used them for guarding and doing pickets.

The next morning we started off and that evening succeeded in getting safely through the most dangerous part, for the enemy had concealed pickets and did patrols regularly, ever on the watch should the British advance that way. But we got through not only without striking a blow, but, we also hoped, without their knowledge—this last point being most important, for they would never give us rest night or day, if they knew we were behind their lines.

As we were ignorant of the nature of the country we relied entirely upon information received from the natives, who in these parts were even friendlier than before. They never gave us away, supplied us with guides and kept us well in touch with the enemy's movements. On the third day we came to a wild and thinly inhabited country, where parties of Germans were looting any cattle they could find. We managed to evade these parties successfully and next day, as our food had run short, we had also to depend on the unfortunate natives who gave us what we wanted gladly,

K

seeming indifferent as to whether they received
payment or not ; but on this trip we were supplied
with money from G.H.Q., and according to orders
were most particular to pay for everything we
had, in new English rupee pieces. Although the
natives had never seen the coin before, they never-
theless readily understood when I explained to
them that these rupees were exactly the same value
as the German silver rupee, but instead of having
the Kaiser Wilhelm's head they had that of King
George, who was King of all the English and master
of the great army which was slowly creeping
forward through the land, driving the Germans
before it, until soon there would not be a single
German left in their country.

The old Jumbi of the village and his son, to
whom I was speaking, were greatly impressed and
the old man said :—

" And does King George ride at the head of his
great army on a white donkey, as I once saw a
German commander do at Dar-es-Salaam ? "

" No," said I.   " He does not ride with them,
yet he knows what they are doing all the same."

" Oh, yes," said the younger man, " I know,
King George rides above in that four-winged
bird which we see coming over sometimes and
making a loud noise. The Germans took my
brother to be a porter and the other day, when he
ran away and came home, he told me that the
four-winged bird's eggs are terrible when it lays
them on the German camp, for they explode and
kill people and a piece of egg shell hit my brother's
friend on the head and he died. Yes, I always had

my thoughts that it was only a king who could manage so formidable a bird."

" No," said I, " you are quite wrong. The king does not fly above in the bird to watch his armies. In fact he is not even in this country, he is home in *Ulaya* (England)."

" Oh ! " said both men in surprise. " How is it that his army is out here fighting ? "

" Well, you see, General Smuts, one of his generals living in another of his territories, was called up to take charge of the King's armies fighting in this land ; for the King has also many other armies fighting against the Germans near *Ulaya*, and the war is much bigger out there and they are fighting much more fiercely there than here. Do you see all those heads of green *mtama* (native grain) in that field of yours over there ? Well, the grain in them is not so numerous as the King's soldiers fighting in *Ulaya*. Then look at those few heads by themselves at the corner of the field, which the baboons have pulled down. Those are only as the men fighting out here, yet no doubt you have heard the English are many even here ? "

" Yes, we have heard they look like a swarm of locusts coming on in the distance."

" So you see that King George could not find time to ride ahead of his little army out here, even if he wanted to."

" Then," the young man said, " I suppose Bwana Mkubwa Smutsie rides on the great bird over his armies and drops the eggs on the Germans ? "

" No, General Smuts does not go up regularly

in the bird, for he is very busy organizing below
and sends his lieutenants up. He generally rides
in a motor car when he wants to visit the front."

"Yes," said the old man approvingly, "that is
a much better thing to ride in than on the back of
a donkey or a bird which might let him drop. I
know a motor car is very fast though I have not
seen one yet—I have only seen the bird. Is it as
fast as the bird ? "

Conversation was here interrupted by a very
wrinkly old woman and her daughter bringing
along three large pumpkins, a chicken and a small
basket of meal, which they had just been grinding
between two stones. The Jumbi stood up saying :—

"Take this offering from a poor man, for you
are our new masters. I only wish it could have
been more. We *shenzis* of this land must serve
under some white man I know, for I am old and
have learned wisdom. If we black folk were left
to rule ourselves, the strong would eat up the weak,
as of old. We even here have heard much from the
frontier of the justice and prosperity which came
with your King's rule, so might his servants have
success. My son here will guide you safely unto a
certain village, then he will place you in the hands
of another, a friend of ours who knows the country
better farther on, and if you keep a good watch
you may get safely through, for no native of the
wilds will give you Englishmen away. But beware
of those villages near the German camp, for,
although they, too, would gladly help you, they
dare not, because, if it were found out, the Germans
would ravage the village and hang all the elders.

Yes, even I am in danger of my life, for if it were known I gave you these pumpkins I would live not another day."

My two scout companions who did not understand the lingo must have missed a great deal on occasions like this when something—who knows what?—suddenly loosened the tongue of some old native of intellect. Of course, when time permitted I always tried to repeat these conversations to Wienholt and Lewis, but it could not be like hearing them first hand.

Wienholt, who kept the cash, then paid for the foodstuffs and we were prepared to move off, when a native came in looking rather scared and guided us down a hill. We afterwards heard that as we went down the one side of the hill a German patrol came up the other.

The country we passed through for the next six days was greatly disturbed by tribal fighting. Seeing that the Germans were too busily engaged with the English, two tribes had taken full advantage of the opportunity and were raiding each other wholesale. I was told that whole villages in one part had been set on fire at dead of night, and as the inmates came pouring out of their highly inflammable huts, they were clubbed or speared by the raiders. Unfortunate natives came to us with terrible tales of woe and sometimes with more horrible wounds. One man I remember had the skin burnt from his back and a great open sore from the shoulder to the waist, but so animal-like is the African's mentality that he seemed none the worse for his hurts and calmly asked us for medicine.

One day, as we were seated having our morning meal, a mob of cattle suddenly appeared, but went straight on in one direction. We soon realized that they were cattle which had been raided and driven away, and having escaped were now making back for their old home again, in a way cattle often do. Soon came the robbers themselves, a formidable crew, hot on their heels. At the next village there were also lamentations of theft and murder ; but here they seemed more fortunate and only some of the cattle had been stolen and the lads herding murdered. The natives everywhere on seeing we were white men asked that the raiders should be punished, so we did our best to pacify them by explaining that at present the country was in a great state of disorder and we had other work to do first, which was to get information about the Germans ; but as soon as we got back we would inform the Administrative Officer, who would, when these parts fell into our hands, come out with troops to restore order. On going on a little further we found that the villages we had passed were most to blame, for they had raided first and the calamity only came upon them in retaliation ; but it was difficult to know whom to believe, for the other side had the same excuse. The country through which we had been passing had been in former times a neutral belt between two tribes.

The next day as we were marching over some flat country we came upon the advance guard of a party of some hundred and fifty Masai warriors on the war path, all carrying long-bladed spears and gaily painted shields, with short swords at their sides, sheathed in scabbards dyed scarlet, while their well-greased bodies were adorned with fantastic markings and their heads with ostrich feathers. Some of the men also carried old-fashioned muzzle-loader guns. As they saw us advancing they evidently thought we had come to deal out punishment, and in spite of our calling to them to stop, for we had been wanting to get a guide, they dashed off into the bush, only one young warrior more bold than the rest remaining in a crouched position looking at us from behind his shield, not fifty yards away. As Wienholt and I went up to him, asking the man with gestures and a friendly voice to come near, he also made off, and with two bounds was hidden in the bush, and where only a few minutes ago stood the band of warriors, now was silence, so completely had they slunk away and hidden themselves. We marched on rather disappointed, as we had been unable to get a guide owing to the unsettled nature of all the villages, each man being too busy protecting his own property or intent on raiding that of his neighbours to come with us.

All that day and half the next we travelled through flat bush-covered, uninhabited country, and the day after we realized we were quite lost, with no water to be found anywhere. Wienholt, who could sometimes be most cheerful when things went wrong, said :—

" Well, I am sure the Germans don't know where we are, anyhow, for we don't know ourselves ! "

CHAPTER XVII

THE DESTRUCTIVE BABOONS

THE next day, following a small native track, we came upon a little group of villages from which we obtained food and guides and also heard that on some of the high peaks there were German pickets, who had piled up firewood ready for a warning beacon should the British advance in that direction.

We were glad to see the villages around these parts were peaceful and undisturbed by tribal fighting, being too far from the Masai border. Later, crossing a fairly large stream, we saw on every side ripe grain (mostly *mtama*) waving in the breeze, but the natives seemed to be having great trouble from baboons, a large mob of which scuttled off from a *mtama* field as we came along. In these parts the loathsome animals were possessed of enormous cheek and regarded us defiantly from only fifty paces away, coming back to their work of destruction immediately we passed on. Their method was to climb up the stalk of the native corn and as it bent over or broke down under their weight, they would hurriedly tear off the grain and force it into their cheek pouches.

A little farther on we camped and I left my companions to try and get some guinea-fowl with my miniature rifle. These, however, made off and I watched a poor unfortunate grey-haired man trying to keep a plague of baboons from his patch of cultivation. He was having a pretty rotten time, for the baboons were all around him. When he went to the one side of the field the baboons would come in and steal on the other side and I could see it was only a matter of a day or two before his crops would be eaten up completely, if he did not adopt some other method. Yet he kept up his cursing and futile waving of sticks which the animals seemed to heed but very little.

I walked down to the field and as the baboons saw a second man coming along they drew off a bit.

" Good morning, father, you are having a pretty rough time with these animals ? "

The old man turned his wizened old face towards me and going down on his knees " Jambo'ed " respectfully and at once took up the tale of woe.

" Yes, the baboons in these parts are getting worse and worse every year, and I don't know what is to become of us. Before I did not fear them, for my two sons, sturdy lads, with sticks, stones and arrows kept off the animals : but now the boys have both gone—both gone," repeated the old man sadly. " The eldest ran away and joined the army. He had had his head filled with madness by a native recruiting sergeant who passed through this way. When he went I only had one left who was old enough to help me and my feeble old wife in the field. Then a year ago he, too, was dragged from us by the Germans ; but this time forcibly, to carry their loads, so this season I am left only with my youngest, a boy of about ten. When the crops ripened he with a stout stick stood at the far end of the field and I sat this end weaving baskets to store the grain in, and the baboons, finding it hopeless left our little patch alone and went to larger fields, but only three days ago the lad was at his post when a huge male baboon, bigger than the boy himself, rushed at him and bit at his arm with its terrible fangs, nearly baring the bone. The lad is with his mother in the hut and on the point of death. This season I am afraid we shall starve, for, see—they have almost finished my crop already. Watch the cunning devils now. As there are two of us they are keeping at a safe distance. That big fellow in the front is the one who bit my boy. Will not the white man shoot him, for he leads the others on to wickedness and makes them bold ? One day they will attack me."

" Yes, I will shoot him in a minute ; but first we will go and see what we can do for the boy."

Coming to a little round hut, I entered a door not two feet high and stood up inside a neat, but smoke-smelling apartment. At my elbow I heard a low moaning and as my eyes became accustomed to the light I saw the bright eyes of the lad fixed on me. He was lying on some skins, while perspiration poured from his brow owing to sheer pain, from which he appeared to be almost delirious. A very wrinkled grey-haired old woman bent over him, trying to comfort her child. I gave the old man some permanganate, instructing him to wash the wound regularly with the disinfectant in hot water. I then told him to remain behind as I walked down to the little patch of cultivation. About twenty baboons of various sizes—some enormous, some only babies riding on their mother's back, others only half-grown—were intent on devouring the old man's crops and took very little notice of me as I came towards them. The big male defiantly looked at me in a threatening manner now, not twenty yards away. He had evidently not seen a white man's gun before. I took careful aim and got the old fellow through the head. So little noise did the small .22 rifle make and so quietly did the big baboon sink down that I succeeded in killing two more before they found out what was happening and I wounded a fourth as they made off. I followed the mob some distance in the bush and got another shot ; but by now the animals, having discovered the danger, made off with all speed, so I returned to the old native telling him to prop up the dead baboons on sticks around his cultivation and he would be troubled no more for this season.

I had a good look at the giant baboon and he truly was a formidable creature, twice the size of any of the others, almost grey in colour. He had a powerfully built body and great jaws with fangs two inches long.

The old native was most grateful and became quite chatty, explaining how this same baboon had also killed his dog, by getting a hold on its neck, then with all four feet which are also hands, forcing the body from him and tearing away about a pound of flesh, so that the unfortunate animal soon bled to death.

I then returned to camp, finding the others saddled up and ready to start. Wienholt had succeeded in getting some more native meal and pumpkins, which were very welcome as we were literally starving. The guide took us on until we came to some very rugged, hilly country which, though beautiful to look at, presented the problem as to how we were to get on, and the following day was spent in getting the mules either up or down some precipitous ridge. That evening we camped on the top of one of the beautiful wooded crests, and as I was doing a little reconnoitring, only a short distance from the camp, I came upon two magnificent black and white sable antelope, standing as high as a large ox and with long horns sweeping in a curve backwards. They stood regarding me for a time, then bounded away with extraordinary lightness for so large a beast. Although I should have liked to have killed one of the animals for the friendly village nearby, I dare not fire a shot as on any of these peaks there might be lurking a German picket.

The next day the guide took us down the side of the mountain and we found ourselves wading ankle deep on the flat surface of a sandy bedded stream. It was a great comfort to be striding along on level ground again and I am sure our mules also appreciated the change. All that day we marched onwards in our watery path, winding through the deep cutting, with mountains rising high on either side. If we had not been guided to this particular path we should never have been able to get through with the pack animals. At one place the narrow valley opened and there clustered a little village, with sugar cane growing right up the banks of the stream, and at sight of it we all seemed to have a sort of sugar hunger, an overwhelming craving for something sweet. This was due, no doubt, to the prolonged lack of sugar in our diet. We bought some of the cane and all walked along munching and sucking the juice with great satisfaction.

The next day the mountains fell away on either side and we came out on open country, eventually sighting the Wami River, a broad stream infested with crocodiles. According to our calculations the British army should be at the crossing, only some five miles down stream, but somehow something must have gone wrong, for although we had been making careful enquiries from the natives on the way, no definite news of our column could be obtained. The last native I had questioned had said there was a vague rumour that the British army was still very far back and the Germans were shelling it vigorously with their big guns, which could be heard for miles—as fast as the British came forward they were blown to pieces. The man who had told my informant had actually heard the guns for two weeks on end without ceasing. I could see at once that the last rumour was merely one of those which travel so quickly amongst native tribes and generally become enormously exaggerated, though with sometimes a meagre foundation of truth, so I only interpreted to my companions that part which I thought most likely to be true.

The three of us discussed the situation long over our midday meal of boiled pumpkins and native porridge, and we decided that the British column must have been held up. The situation was by no means a pleasant one, for there were we, some seventy miles behind the German lines, and immediately between us and our own people lay Von Lettow, camped at a place called Turiani, with his great army of mustered strength. To add to our danger we were now practically right on the German lines of communication which were sure to be guarded, for only some five miles away was the great road which fed the German camp with supplies from the Central railway. Besides, as the natives had the rumours that our forces were far away and being blown to pieces, it was quite possible some of them, seeking a fat reward from the Germans, would now give us British away.

We had all been having a lot of fever of late and with the constant watching, uncertainty and broken sleep I suppose our nerves were torn thin, so our discussion, which started in a friendly council of war, finished up in a quarrel between Wienholt and myself, for we both looked upon the situation from a different view point. The source of the trouble, of course, was with our chief at G.H.Q., who was in the habit of sending us out, three Intelligence Agents of exactly the same rank, without declaring which was to be officially in charge. On the two previous trips things had generally worked well, for the three of us understood each other and took up our various duties automatically. Wienholt generally wrote out and made up the reports and sent them in to H.Q. by a native when we got a chance ; he also, being very keen and conscientious, generally supplied most of the push, and I doubt if we should have got as far as we did if it had not been for his tenacity. Lewis generally took on the job of looking after the pack animals and askaris, as he suffered a great deal from malaria and was glad to take things quietly. I, having long experience of Africa and being able to speak the native language fluently, spent my time foraging for information, which was merely a matter of tactfully speaking to the natives, and then explaining the situation to my two companions, when we would discuss the position as quickly as we could and decide upon a plan of action. As Wienholt was a very much older man than myself I generally gave in to his views, as they were so reasonable and often so obviously the right thing to do, but on this occasion we quarrelled. I had just had a long conversation with a native, who was employed by a German in charge of the ordinance magazine at the river crossing, where the temporary grass buildings were stacked full of provisions and ammunition and other sinews of war. I had questioned the native most carefully and there was only the white German in charge with two askaris. There would be nothing easier, I explained, than to cross the river with a canoe under cover of the night, overpower the German and his askaris, loot any valuables we might desire for ourselves and take what food our men could carry, then set fire to all the buildings, which were said to contain a colossal amount of stores, and get back across the river as quickly as possible and lose ourselves in the bush. But Weinholt, who did not get the news first hand,

seemed to think there must be a catch in it, so he
insisted that before deciding on anything we must
discuss his plan, which was to hold up a German
ration convoy going to the front from the magazine.
He emphasized the point that it was a great disadvantage to get across to the other side of the river
and we were not certain there was not a whole
company guarding the depot.

I pointed out that it would be most difficult to
destroy any rations on transit, except comparatively
small quantities, and it would be much easier to
burn them while massed in inflammable thatched
buildings.   But Weinholt seemed to scent danger
somewhere and held out more obstinately than I
had ever known him to do before, so in the end I
left him and Lewis in disgust and going out into
the night lay down in some bushes and long grass
a little distance away to rest, and perhaps brood
over the imaginary grievance.

I again went over in my mind every word the
native had said.   Yes, my plan was obviously
easier ; we would commence operations to-night
instead of in the morning and would do a vast deal
more damage.   Some hours later I arose and went
back to find my companions had already turned
in for the night, but Weinholt was still awake
waiting for me and in whispers he again discussed
the problem, but had entirely changed his tactics,
for he started by apologizing for some of our first
argument, until I could no longer resist his slow
persistence and he gained his point.

Looking at the incident afterwards I am sure he
was right, as it would have been a risky thing to

have a river like the Wami between us, when pursued, as crossings could not always readily be
found.

We arose very early the next morning and I had
another chat with the villager employed by the
German supply officer across the river, and he went
along with us for a short way—then struck off
towards the river, saying he must not be late, for
his master was very strict and ready with the
kiboko.

CHAPTER XVIII

A HOLD-UP ON THE HIGHWAY

WE left the small native path we had been following and going through some bush country came out right on the main road. It was a broad one, newly made and, as we could see, constantly used, although just at the moment there was nothing in sight. So we crossed over and continued our journey on the other side until we reached some native huts, where we ate beautiful ripe paw-paws from the trees as we discussed the latest news with the villagers.

No, they had not heard of the English column as yet ; but some of their friends living further on had heard the bombarding of many guns for weeks.

Just then through the scattered trees and long grass we saw a small convoy of pack donkeys, in charge of a Greek or two, followed by hundreds of natives carrying loads on their heads. As we watched there seemed no end to the long line, which appeared to stretch out for miles. We let the first lot of askaris and pack donkeys go past and when they were out of sight we cut in upon the road, finding only one remaining askari in charge. He must have thought we were Germans, for as we came up he stood and waited, making no attempt to flee or defend himself, so we walked right up to him, and Weinholt relieved him of his rifle, which he handed over quite willingly. By this time there was quite a little knot of carriers standing before us and, being the spokesman, I thought it about time we commenced, so addressed them as one giving an order, saying :—

" Now, do you hear all of you ? Throw down your loads over there and then go and fetch fire-wood. There are plenty of cut trees and scrub lying in heaps on either side of the road."

The natives, being accustomed to obey the words of a white man, immediately did exactly as I told them. I could feel I had their confidence and soon we had a huge blaze. As fresh niggers came along each man heaved his load into the fire and hastened off for firewood. So many loads were thrown in that at last we found in spite of the size of the fire, which now had flames reaching twelve feet high, it was in danger of being extinguished, so I ordered that the bags of grain and meal were to be ripped open and scattered on the ground, while other things more inflammable, such as brown sugar and packages of clothes, were heaved into the fire. There is nothing, we found, like bags of brown sugar for making a blaze.

Wienholt, as soon as we had arrived on the road, went after some of the porters who had gone on, quite blissfully, not knowing what was happening behind, and, cursing and swearing at them in German, he made them also come back with their loads, which were promptly thrown on to the fire.

I shall never forget this burning of the German provisions. For days we had been existing in a state of semi-starvation and now here was a mountain of food before us. I took in one hand a great bunch of German sausages and while directing operations, munched great mouthfuls and then went on to brown sugar, a clammy lump of which I had forced into each pocket. Lewis and our men soon joined in the feast too, and I invited the German porters to follow suit, telling them they could eat as much as they liked provided they did not carry anything away, and they seemed to relish the sugar more than anything. The only one who stood aloof was the German askari, who bore a troubled and sullen look. Then Wienholt came back, and I greeted him with :—

" Have a sausage, Arnold ? I have just eaten twelve and two lumps of sugar."

I handed him the basket of particularly choice cooked sausages meant for G.H.Q., into which I had been dipping regularly ; but my companion was in a serious frame of mind and his face wore a set expression as he said severely :—

" We must not eat raw sausages, they will be sure to bring out the fever. Besides, we have not cut the telegraph wires yet."

" Have a hot roasted one, then," said I, pointing to a great cluster of the more common variety, which a German porter was grilling at the end of a long stick. But Wienholt did not comply, seeming displeased at our jollifications and proceeded to cut the telegraph wire, which in the excitement we had overlooked.

All this feasting and the hot fire, as well as the pepper and spice in the sausages, brought on a terrible thirst, and as Wienholt was the only one who could read German, I asked him what the contents of two cases were, which we had spared from the flames. Reading the labels he said the one contained *Schnapps* and the other case something else which I cannot remember. I did not like the sound of either, still less the smell of the stuff in the bottles, so I took a long draught of water from my water bottle instead and instructed a native to smash all the bottles with an axe. Then as Wienholt and Lewis, with the help of some willing hands, were busy pulling down a telegraph pole, I addressed the gathering throng of German porters before me, about two hundred in all. I told them that we were English and would now continue our journey, having destroyed our enemy's loads. They must not go back to their German masters, but they had our permission to return to their own homes.

Most of them complained that their homes were very far away and they wanted to go on with us.

" We want you to be our masters," they said, while two or three older and less adventurous spirits said they would go home if I gave them a barua (letter) to safeguard them on the journey, but otherwise they would also prefer to come with us.

I explained that it would not be wise for so large a crowd of unarmed men to come with us, as we were a long distance from our own people and between us lay waiting a great gathering of the enemy, to deal vengeance for this destruction of their food. We English scouts in enemy country

relied entirely for our safety upon the mobility and
smallness of our numbers and we would have to
creep stealthily back as we had come. However,
I agreed to take back three men to help carry the
provisions we had just captured. Then looking
about me I picked out three of the best looking
men I could find, and two of our pack mules also
having been loaded up with provisions, we marched
on. But so eager were all the German porters to
come with us that many of them followed, and we
had to threaten violence before they were dis-
couraged and went back sadly to the road again.

I felt very sorry for the poor fellows, who no
doubt would have to face the vengeance of their
German masters, but what were we to do ? They
would fare far worse if they came with us, for they
would be sure to be captured and probably shot
down at sight, as it would be impossible to steer
back safely so unwieldy an unarmed mob.

CHAPTER XIX

WIENHOLT TAKEN PRISONER

IN another half-hour we were lost in the trackless wilderness of thornbush and marched on steadily, parallel with the Wami River. That night we obtained water from a backwash of the river, which, owing to the flat nature of the country in these particular parts, ran back over a mile. Early the next morning we pushed on again for mile after mile, forcing our way through matted grass shoulder high. We had now left the bush country for the great plains stretching away on either side of the river, dotted only here and there with tall palms and covered by this almost impenetrable grass, which more resembled reeds in nature.

That evening to get water we cut in towards the river and came upon a native village, the occupants of which all appeared friendly. They told us they had seen nothing of the Germans, and the Jumbi agreed to supply us with a guide the next morning, so we gave him a great lump of sugar. Then finding a suitable place about half a mile from the village, we cooked our food and according to our custom when out scouting in dangerous country, made all preparations after the meal as if to camp for the night, but instead of doing so moved off again after dark for a mile or so, where we hid ourselves in the bush and long grass and there made the true camp.

Towards morning I was awakened by Wienholt whispering in my ear, saying he heard someone in the distance whistling as if to locate us. The hour was just before dawn, but a bright full moon shining made the night almost as bright as day. After hastily exchanging views we decided that it must be our guide from the village. Still there was something strange about the whole thing, for he was not expected so early and did not know we had moved camp. So it was decided that Lewis and I were to saddle up the mules and get everything ready for a hasty retreat, while Wienholt went forward to locate the whistler. Hardly had he gone two minutes when a burst of firing started in the direction he had taken, and a regular fusillade soon poured into our camp. The enemy were evidently right upon us, but not quite sure of our position. Everyone was awake by now and Lewis and I arranged the men ready to receive an attack. I told the captured porters and the mule boys to lie down and take cover, but be ready to retire immediately we did so. Then we waited another five minutes for Wienholt to come back, but there was no sign of him, and as the enemy were still firing in the direction of our camp, now from a much closer range and in great numbers, we decided we must retreat.

We felt convinced that Wienholt had either been killed or captured. To strengthen this last view Lewis said he distinctly heard Wienholt's voice calling out to us the words : " Get out of it, boys ! "

This, however, must have been a delusion or the voice of some German commander, for six months later, when Wienholt escaped, he said he had not called out at all, but dodged the enemy by making for the river in the other direction.

I was just deciding on the best direction to take when our askari prisoner, finding himself unguarded for a moment, made a dash for freedom and in the very direction I had in my mind fixed upon for our retreat. Hardly had he gone twenty yards, however, when he fell to the ground, shot by a further party of Germans closing in on our flank, and his fate would also have been ours if I had taken that direction. There was now only one way open for us and we took it. Lewis, myself, one askari and the three captured German porters got out safely. All the others were either killed or became so panic stricken that they ran blindly on and got lost in the bush.

As soon as we had got safely about a mile away, we hid in a patch of long grass and waited some time in case Wienholt or any of the stragglers should come along ; but we saw nobody and, fearing that the enemy, who were in considerable numbers, would send out small search parties, we went on. We were now almost destitute, in the hurry of the last moments having escaped with only what we stood up in, which was the clothes we were wearing, rifles and ammunition ; we had not a bite of food, nor a drop of water between us. The lack of water concerned us more than anything, for the sun was already beginning to scorch down upon our heads and we had a long dry stretch before us. We had

neither map, compasses nor guide and were in a
strange land, so could only take the direction we
thought best.   Fortunately I had so often looked at
the map that I had the lay of the land clearly
impressed upon my memory.

Next day when we came in sight of a distant peak
about forty miles away, one of the German porters
said that it was the mountain under which the great
German army lay waiting, so I at once knew it
must be the high peak on the Kanga Mountains,
lying beyond the German camp Turiani, and with
such a landmark in sight there was no reason why
we should not steer a fairly accurate course towards
our own camp ; but we should have to act with
great caution, for we well knew Von Lettow would
not easily let us return unmolested, after so impu-
dently destroying his valuable supplies.

For three days we travelled on, never daring to
use even the smallest native track, but always
forcing a way for ourselves through the long dry
grass, which grew in endless quantities on that hot
and parched plain.

We suffered terribly from thirst at times, but
always seemed to find water at the last moment,
just as we were giving up all hope.   We trusted no
natives and gave any villagers we saw in the day-
time a wide berth, or hid in the grass until nightfall,
and then, when the neighbourhood seemed free of
the enemy, we would stealthily enter the village
under cover of the darkness, just at a time when
the natives would be having their evening meal.
We would take possession of all the food we could

see, drain their water jars and disappear again in the long grass, as mysteriously as we had come.

We crossed several German roads, including a large one with telephone wires, and every day came upon signs of the enemy. One day while hiding near a German path our only remaining askari, whom we had set to watch the road and who had become very jumpy of late, owing to our experiences, suddenly got up and ran away into the bush, as if the very devil were at his heels. I sent one of the German porters after him, but the askari ran blindly on and was lost in the bush. We found the cause of his alarm was a body of askaris marching along the path ; but they passed on quite unconscious of our presence.

Our party was now reduced to five—Lewis, myself and the three German porters, who stuck to us most faithfully—and as we were both weak from fever they took it in turns to walk in front and force the long and tangled grass apart so that the rest of us might pass along easily. Thus we walked wearily on, day after day, through an endless sea of tall grass, the monotony of the plains only broken by a tall palm here and there, or some native or German track crossing our path.

One day we came upon a deep sluggish river, a tributary of the Wami and also infested with crocodiles. We feared we should have to swim across as there seemed no other way of getting over, but fortunately we captured a lonely native and he guided us to a bridge quite near at hand, formed by a huge tree trunk which had fallen right across the channel. All the next day we were unable to find water, although we travelled farther than we had ever done before, owing to the nature of the country having now changed to open bush and fairly short grass. That night we went to rest very thirsty and by midday the following day we became desperate. We came upon a large native village but found all the inhabitants had been removed and an enemy picket put on the village water-hole, I suppose to make doubly sure we should receive no assistance here. The grass and bushes grew fairly thick all around so we were able to lurk about quite close without being seen. We worked our way right to the barricade of cut trees surrounding the cultivated land and huts and there I caught sight of the only living creature our enemies had left, a very old man with grey head and white beard, sitting at the entrance of one of the huts weaving a grass mat. A sudden idea came to me, for here was someone who might know of other water in the neighbourhood besides that held by the German picket, so in a few strides I was through the gap in the fence and had crossed the ground between us and the hut, seized the old man by the wrist, jerked him to his feet and before he knew what was happening he was hurried back to our hiding-place, seized by two sturdy German porters, and we all hurried off with our prey to the depths of the bushes and long grass. Making sure we were out of earshot of the picket, I started to question the old man about water, but he remained sullen, pretending he did not understand what I said. I had my suspicions that he merely did this to get out of the trouble of taking us to water, but a burning thirst was raging within me and I said, I suppose with meaning in my voice, that if he did not show us where water was at once we would cut his throat, drain him of his life blood and drink that. Even this fierce threat had little effect and he said something about our already having possession of the water and having taken away and killed or worked to death his sons and grandsons, now we could kill him if we liked. Being so desperate with thirst I could no longer think logically but fell upon the old man and thumped his frail old body around the clearing without mercy. At last he held his hand up begging me to cease and he would show us where the water was. He then feebly led the way through the bush and I walked behind him with the barrel of my rifle between his shoulders, ready to deal justice should he prove treacherous and betray us. Silently the little procession went onward and at last the old man stood still and looked down at a moist patch of earth, saying the water there was not good but there was no other.

We needed no second bidding and the three porters soon scooped out a hole in the ground a foot deep, while we kept watch for the enemy. To our great joy the hollow began to fill up with water, but it was of a peculiar whitish colour and tasted very strongly of some unknown mineral properties. However, everyone drank his fill and we also filled up a small calabash we had found at one of the villages, marched on for half a mile and then hid in the bush for we could go no farther. Soon after this Lewis and I were taken with violent ague and sickness, which we put down to something in the water bringing out malaria. By evening, however, we felt a little better and determined to do a night march as this area seemed particularly well guarded by the enemy.

The next question was what to do with the old man, for if we let him go back he would immediately tell the Germans the direction we had taken, though, on the other hand, if we took him with us he might retard our progress, being old and feeble. I went over to where he was seated on the ground with the other three natives and to my surprise found him chatting away to them quite amicably. As I came up he arose nimbly to his feet, greeting me with "Jambo, Bwana!" all his decrepitude having disappeared, and, as I put the question which was concerning me, to my further surprise Grandpa, as Lewis and I called him, said he could walk as well as we and wanted to come along with us.

It appeared he had learnt from the other natives that we were British and had no intentions of taking him off to carry heavy loads.

That night we did not cover a great distance owing to the darkness of the night and the nature of the country which was covered with high grass. We hid ourselves at about midnight and slept undisturbed until the morning. The evening before we had heard the distant booming of the heavy German guns, evidently firing at a very long range, for the sound of the shells bursting was heard long after the shot was fired. This morning the sound was much nearer, and as the shelling seemed to be kept up regularly every day, we resolved to turn the sound to our own advantage, for it was obvious that where we heard the shells burst was the British camp on the Lukiguru River. As we now entered hilly bush country our original landmark was often lost to sight, so the sound of the guns was our only guide.

The next day we were opposite the German camp and only about nine or ten miles from our own, still undiscovered although the Germans had every water-hole they knew of, and even the smallest path, guarded. We did not use the paths, however, but crept forward under cover of the long grass, pushing on when the guns boomed and resting when they stopped ; and in this way, quite independently of landmarks or guides, we were able to take a course with the most cover, avoiding any likely places where the enemy might be lurking. Thus on the sixth day after losing Wienholt on the Wami River we heard the distant hum of a large camp, obviously ours, only it seemed a little too near, for the last shell appeared to have burst a mile or two beyond. So we halted in the long grass to listen for the next one ; but the German gunners seemed to have given up shelling for that day. About half a mile away we saw an outpost on a hill. Was it our people or the enemy ?

We moved forward through some cultivated land. I went on with one of the German porters to try and locate the picket and suddenly came face to face with three or four natives with baskets, peacefully harvesting their crops. I asked them if the outpost on the hill was German or English. They regarded me suspiciously and backing away

said :—" It is a German picket,"—at the same time
starting to slink off.

As I saw they were getting further and further
from me, I commanded them to stop ; but on hearing my voice they threw away their baskets and ran
like hares towards the hill, loudly calling for help
in Swahili :—

" Askari, askari, hapa wadui ! " (Soldier, soldier
here is the enemy.)

It was now too obvious that we had almost run
our noses into an enemy's camp and in no time
the troops on the hill would come swarming down
to hunt us, so the German porter and I ran as fast
as the natives, but in the opposite direction and,
joining up with Lewis and the others, we all took
to our heels. Lewis and I, being weighed down by
rifle and ammunition, soon got left behind. I
noticed a hiding-place at the edge of the cultivation,
a fallen tree covered by thick matted creepers, so
dived into this. Lewis came in after me and the
two of us crouched down ready with our rifles
should the enemy come along to look for us.

For an hour we lay thus, but nothing stirred and
I was beginning to think that perhaps after all the
camp was British. It struck me that perhaps the
natives we had met, mistaking us for Huns, had
said the picket was German just to please us and
gain time until they were a safe distance off, when
I thought I had heard one of them shouting back
at us defiantly : " English ! "

I explained my theory to Lewis and told him
we had best get along and try to work around
the outpost and obtain more information, but the

HOW THE E.A.M.R. CAMOUFLAGED WHITE PONIES TO LOOK LIKE ZEBRA IN THE BUSH

[p. 115.

MEN OF THE E.A.M.R. WATCH THE FIRST AEROPLANE TO FLY IN
KENYA AT MBUYUNI

[p. 120.

excitement had brought out fever in him again, so I had to go on alone. I told Lewis to remain where he was and, if I got to the camp safely and it was British, I would come back for him ; otherwise he would know I had been captured.

Under cover of the grass I very cautiously worked around the picket only to find another. This I also managed to evade and at last got right past the chain of outposts and only about a mile or so from a large camp, hidden in the trees, which I could distinctly hear from my hiding-place.

Was it a British or a German camp ?

I decided to lie concealed until I saw some stragglers, who would be sure to pass that way sooner or later. I waited for several hours then heard loud guttural voices coming from the other side of the bush, quite near, and a minute later six men rode past me. My heart sank, for sure enough each man carried a Mauser rifle and the guttural tone was unmistakable, although they wore khaki shirts and helmets very much like our men. I crouched low and when the men had passed I gave one look around to see if all was clear, then moved stealthily back—now just as eager to get out of that chain of pickets as I had been to get in.

Under cover of the long grass I was just creeping past the first outpost when I got a full view of one of the men and recognized the uniform of our 29th Punjabis. I called out : " Don't shoot ! " and walked up to him, trying to explain who I was and how I had got there, but nobody understood English, not even the Sergeant in charge.

Although they were courteous I could see they

M

regarded me with great suspicion, and I did not blame them either, for my uniform was in such a dilapidated, torn and filthy state that no self-respecting British soldier would easily claim me as a comrade. I was taken along under escort to the Punjabis' Colonel and as I neared the camp I again came upon troops armed with Mausers and talking in that suspicious guttural tongue. The mystery which had been greatly troubling me was solved, for I found that since my absence a corps of local Uasin Gishu Boers had joined our forces and for some unknown reason were armed with Portuguese Mauser rifles, which are almost identical with those of the Germans. We soon arrived at the Punjabis lines and I explained matters to the Colonel, but he was not satisfied, especially when he heard I had come in from the enemy's lines, and must have thought me a spy, for he took the precaution of sending an officer along with me to I.D. Head-quarters. Here several of my comrades rushed out to meet me, thinking our party had been long since wiped out. I was received as one returning from the dead.

CHAPTER XX

THE END OF A LONG, HAZARDOUS JOURNEY

FOOD was hurriedly brought and I had the first decent meal since we were attacked on the Wami. Then came an urgent message from G.H.Q. ordering me to report at once. I arose and staggered forward. Now that I was safe in camp something inside seemed to give way and for the first time I realized how weak I was. With great efforts I at last managed to reach G.H.Q.—walking fairly straight ; but I could feel the fever coming on. The great feed had evidently done the trick. I felt I must somehow keep going until I got this interview over and had found Lewis, after which I could lie down and be as ill as I liked.

I discovered that our original G.S.O.3., Capt. Dickenson, a regular officer of fine type, who knew his job and understood us, had been sent back with fever and I had to go and see another officer who seemed to be in a blue funk about sending in false information to the General. On giving in my report he stopped me at a certain passage saying, in the manner some school mistress would use to a small boy, telling her a rather tall yarn :—

" And what river did you say you got to ? "

" The Wami, sir," said I.

" But," said the staff officer indicating the map
spread out before us : " The Wami is over there—
let me see—at least sixty miles from here and fifty
miles behind the German lines. Von Lettow's
camp lies over there between us and the Wami.
Do you happen to know that ? "

" Well, we went around it, sir," said I, now,
I am afraid, rather curtly ; for malaria will upset
the temper of the most placid and just at the moment
I felt as if the fires of hell itself were burning inside
me and then as if I were standing on air, lifted off
my feet and suspended by some unknown hand.

" Don't you think it was some other river you
went to, say the Lukiguru, a little lower down,
for instance ? "

" No, it was the Wami.   But, sir, I am afraid I
shall have to ask you to allow me to sit down, for
I am very ill."

But the officer before me did not seem to hear,
being deeply engrossed in the map, so I had to
remain standing.

After some meditation he said :

" Now let me see, how many German loads did
you say you destroyed ? "

" About two hundred, sir."

" Two hundred ?   And only three of you with
four askaris ?   Did you bring back any natives who
might corroborate this information ?   You say all
your askaris were killed in action, or lost in the
bush.   You know I must be very careful not to give
in false information.   You understand my position,
don't you ? "

I said as civilly as I could to the officer :—

" No, I don't, sir.   Our former Chief, who sent us out on this trip, did not need corroboration by natives.   I have given you my report and you can take it for what it is worth.   Now, may I go and find my comrade, Lewis, who is lying out on the veldt pretty bad with fever ? "

Just as I was leaving the banda General Hoskins came in.   My heart sank within me, for it meant going over the whole interview a second time.   But the General readily saw my plight and when I told him I had just given in my report he allowed me to go.

I went back to the I.D. Headquarters and there three other agents, Duirs, Jenkins and Middleton, were ready to accompany me back to find Lewis. We rode out on mules and I was so bad with fever by now that one of my companions had to ride on either side to prevent me from falling out of the saddle.   At last we reached the place, but Lewis was not there.   The disappointment was very great, for I was afraid he had taken fright and thinking me captured had gone off into the bush, perhaps to die of thirst.

I told my companions I could do no more— they would just have to search around themselves, and I slid down from the saddle and lay on the ground in a semi-conscious state.   Then an idea came to me—Lewis might be hiding near by afraid to expose himself, thinking that we were the enemy, and if we could only give him some sign of our presence he would come out at once.   So I told Jenkins, being from Australia like Lewis, to give the bushman's " Coo-ee " and half an hour later

Lewis was found. Having, it appeared, heard a shot a short time after I left him, and thinking I had run into the picket and the worst had happened, he had decided to shift to a safer hiding-place. He was feeling much better and was, of course, greatly relieved to meet us all again.

My fever was becoming worse and worse, in fact I remember little of the trip back to camp, except that I was put on a mule and held there by two of my friends. When we got back, Duirs, one of my old scout companions, went to the hospital asking them to send out a stretcher for me, but was told the hospital was so full that there was not a square inch to spare, also that the doctor was too busy to come and see me.

In the afternoon I came to myself again. The fever for a time was over and the burning temperature had gone off leaving me very weak. I tried to get some rest, but high explosive shells from the German naval guns started bursting over our camp; so with the assistance of a comrade I staggered to the dug-out, to find all the others down there. There is nothing which jars on the nerves of a sick man more than the bursting of shells, especially if one has spent weeks of sleepless nights, and I felt miserable, weak and as if all the world was against me. I wished I could again go out into the open wild bush, where I could at least sleep undisturbed and breathe fresh air, instead of being squeezed down in this awful stuffy hole, any moment to be blown up by one of those shells.

For six days had Lewis and I marched, hungry, thirsty and weary—hardly daring to think of the joy of the day when we would get back to our own camp and no longer be harried and hunted. How our Chief would welcome the valuable information we were able to bring back to him ! How he would chuckle approvingly at the way we had burnt the German convoy ! How he would approve of us going on and finding out information after we discovered that we were unsupported by the column !

But instead of all this I had got back to be disbelieved and even insulted—desperately ill, but unable to have medical attention. I shall never forget the despair of this day, so vivid are often the fancies of a man down with fever.

When the Germans ceased shelling I crawled back again to my bed in the banda and later was told that " Grandpa " and the three German porters had turned up in camp and wanted to see me, as they had heard I was very ill. I allowed them to come in and they told me their story.

After they had left us they hid all day and the following day came upon a village, who said that the camp was not German but English, so they came along to find us. I asked the Sergeant in charge of our rations to feed and care for the men well. The food seemed to loosen their tongues and I could hear through the thin walls of the hut the other Intelligence Agents and an officer eagerly questioning them about the German country and they in turn enthusiastically telling their story— how they had thrown their loads in the fire because they wanted to come with the English.

The following day I was strong enough to stagger

to hospital and a day or so later Lewis came to tell me that he had just been informed that the General had greatly appreciated our last exploit and was very glad to grant the three of us, Wienholt, Lewis and myself, a month's extra pay, which meant that we should be credited with £25.

There was a touch of irony in this, for one of us at least. Wienholt, a keen Englishman, thinking only of serving his country in the present time of great crisis, leaving a position of authority, comfort and no doubt luxury on his vast cattle estates in Queensland, had come over here to fight, bringing with him horses and equipment at his own expense —offering to fight without salary—and now, because he had helped to accomplish an extra daring piece of work, he was politely credited with £25 !

CHAPTER XXI

MINE-SWEEPING IN THE BUSH

A FORTNIGHT later I had sufficiently recovered to again take up duties, and this time took out half a dozen askaris to reconnoitre the enemy's outposts. A week later our column at Lukiguru, or " Shell Camp " as it is usually called, was reinforced by large numbers of mounted infantry, and we pushed on to Turiani, which was eventually taken. We halted there for a time, then advanced over the flat country to the Wami River, the enemy now rapidly retiring before us.

On nearing Wami, Duirs and I were sent out with a dozen men and another I.D. agent who had recently joined, to find out information about a force of Germans who were reported to be camped on the banks some ten miles down stream, ready to strike at our lines of communication. We reached the spot indicated, but were unable to find any traces of the enemy, so, according to our orders, would have to cross the river in order to reconnoitre the other side satisfactorily. But how were we to get across ? The water was deep and full of crocodiles and no canoe or boat could be found. We waited until next day in the hope that something might turn up, then decided there was nothing for it but to swim, as we had already delayed too long in searching for a canoe.

The first time I had set eyes on the Wami and its sluggish, scaly reptiles, which could often be seen basking on sandbanks or dozing in the reeds, I had shuddered at the thought of entering its waters. Now circumstances so turned out that we had to swim it and perhaps in the face of the enemy too. However, I was lucky in having such a companion as Duirs, who was a strong and fearless swimmer. We stripped off our clothes, packed them into a kit bag and gave it to a sturdy Kavirondo to bring across safely, knowing the abilities of this tribe in water. Fastening our rifles and cartridge belts to our bodies and choosing a place where a rocky outcrop jutted into the stream, we swam across safely. Just as we reached the far shore an alarm was given and fearing the enemy had been seen on our side of the river, we swam back again as quickly as possible. But imagine our disgust when the agent we had left behind with the askaris said he had merely sighted two natives on his own side. Now we thought we would have to swim the river again, but as circumstances turned out the two natives were able to give us information which saved us this trouble.

After this trip we camped for some days at Dakawa, a crossing on the Wami River, and later pushed on in pursuit of the Germans, who were retiring on the Central railway. A few days after leaving Dakawa, Duirs and I were given another very unpleasant job. The Germans had utilized all the shells which they were unable to fire at Turiani as land mines. In one place the main Morogoro road was so full of mines that our army, after accidentally letting off a few which blew up some of the advance guard, wisely made another track across country to Morogoro Railway Station, and we were to go to the station by the mined road and report on it.

As we made our way along the road we were passed by a Captain of some South African mounted infantry, riding at the head of a troop of men. I questioned a corporal who lagged behind to talk to us and learned that the officer was a Boer from down south and they were on exactly the same errand as ourselves. There had evidently been a mistake in the orders at Headquarters. However, I thought there could be no harm in our Headquarters having two independent reports on so important a subject as a mined road, but the fun would start when we got to the place, for neither party were engineers or had instruments for locating the presence of mines. So far as I could see, about the only way to find a mine was to walk into it and be blown up. Even then we would not be carrying out orders, which were distinctly to report on the road, for how could one make out a report if blown sky high ? It had occurred to me to ask this question when I took my orders that morning, but I refrained from saying anything as my O.C. might think I was funking the job.

We had now reached the mined area and the mounted men, who were going very cautiously only about a quarter of a mile ahead of us, suddenly turned off the road into the bush, as if to avoid

some obstacle. A few minutes later there was a
terrific explosion and a great column of smoke and
dust arose straight up into the air.

" They have found No. 1 for us," said I to Duirs.
" And they are welcome to keep ahead and find all
the others if they like. This is great fun—they go
ahead and let off the mines and we just come along
behind and report on them."

But things did not go as smoothly as this, for the
mounted men had had enough already, and some
of them were seen to be hastening back, covered
from head to foot in spots of filth and blood. Then
came the Boer Captain, limp and carried by two
men. They laid him down near us and I gave him
a drink of water. He was not injured although
covered in blood, and told us his story.

" We were riding along," said he, " when we
came to a place on the road, just over there, where
a mine was exploded yesterday by the advance
guard of the main column. Only a short distance
on was a low barricade. So I thought to myself, if
we touch that barricade another mine will go off,
so I would just be clever and walk my men off the
road at this danger spot and come back again and
report a mine there. But the Germans were much
too slim for us. They had put another mine just
where we would turn out—even cleared a little
path all ready for us to ride in. So hardly had we
gone a few yards when the whole earth seemed to
go up right under a horse just in front of me. The
rider, as well as two others next to him, is lying dead
now. But as I said, the mine went off right under
the horse and blew off both its hind legs. One got

hitched up on a tree about ten feet high, but the other, flying through the air, caught me such a whack at the back of the neck that I was knocked out completely. Oh, my God ! What a headache!" and the unfortunate officer, clasped his hand to his temples and rolled over on the grass.

Duirs and I went on until we came to the place where the tragedy had happened. There we saw a great hole in the ground of newly turned earth and the remains of a horse suspended high up on a tree, where it had caught in a branch. We were just moving forward when another terrific explosion occurred and going forward we met two troopers who were watching the road and they reported that a little distance off they had seen a native dressed in a white Kanzu coming towards them and obviously quite unaware of the mines, when suddenly to their horror he went up in a cloud of smoke, not a particle of his body being seen again.

Our position was a very difficult one, as there were obviously more mines ahead, but how were we to locate them ?

Just then the Boer officer came up, sufficiently recovered to take command. On discussing the problem with him, he told me there was only one way to find the mines and that was to make my unfortunate native porters walk ahead and let them off. Of course I would not allow this and proposed that each party should do a share of the advance guard, but his Sergeant here interrupted saying that at the camp at Dakawa there was a herd of about fifty slaughter oxen. Why not drive these ahead to let off mines ?

" Yes, that is the very thing. I should have thought of it before." And at a word of command all the men mounted their horses and disappeared.

As they could not possibly get back for two days with the oxen, and we were ordered to give an immediate report on the mined road, and then by the next day catch up with the column again, which was now advancing beyond Morogoro, we marched cautiously on along the roadside, making notes of places which looked likely to be mined and the next day came in sight of the township of Morogoro. All the large buildings in the centre of the settlement had enormous red crosses painted on the roofs, I suppose to keep off our aeroplanes, which had been worrying them with bombs a fortnight or so previously.

The Germans had not put up an offensive here but retired southwards, leaving behind all their women and children.

Our forces were now in possession of the only two railways and all the seaport and other towns in the country ; but the enemy forces were still intact and unconquered, retiring southwards, practising guerilla warfare and living on ample stores which they collected from the natives. Although our forces had now taken everything that was worth taking in the country, we still had the arduous task of driving the enemy from those hundreds of miles of endless bush-covered country, some of it thickly populated by natives and therefore well supplied with local foodstuffs.

CHAPTER XXII

ADVENTURE MARCHING ON TULO

WE camped that night a mile beyond Morogoro and next day joined our brigade, which was camped by a small stream some miles further on. Then we all pushed on again, advancing on the German's main camps at Tulo and Magogoni, some forty miles away on the Mruha stream, a tributary of the Ruvu River.

From friendly natives we had learned that the Germans had concentrated stores of foodstuffs and ammunition here and our General meant to try to capture the place, by attacking it from two sides—one force, to which I was attached, keeping to the low country.

The following day I was told off to take charge of the Intelligence work for a party of some two hundred of the 29th Punjabis under a Major James. We were to strike out to the left and wipe up or disperse any enemy outposts and then join the main Punjabi regiment, which would meet us at a certain Mission Station on the Ruvu River. From there we would advance on Tulo and attack it on yet a third side.

This was the first time I was put in charge of the Intelligence work of a force of any size for which

I would be solely responsible, for there was not another man in the party who knew anything about local conditions or a word of the language ; so I felt not a little thrill of pride as I lined up my four dirty ragged askaris and three porters beside the spruce line of Indian regular infantry. The word of command was given and we marched off, I with my four ragamuffins heading the column. Later on when the troops rested and cooked their midday meal I went out to try and get into touch with some villagers. My first concern was to find a guide who knew the country, as the few natives we had passed on the march had been scared into the bush by the sight of so many armed soldiers. I at last succeeded in securing the confidence of some villagers and making friends with them, several offered to guide our party, but I picked out an old man named Brihemu and his son, who said they knew the country as far as the Ruvu River. The column then moved on until late in the afternoon, when as we were about to enter some very rugged, dangerous looking country, hills rising on either side of the road, the O.C. decided that it was not safe to go any farther. I was sent on ahead with my four men, Brihemu and his son leading us along a narrow path running half-way up the slopes overlooking the main path ; but there were no signs of the enemy. Then we went on along more hilly country and about a mile farther on came to a place where the path joined a road and on it we saw the well known hobnail marks made by the German field boot. It was quite evident that a considerable force of the enemy had passed there that very day. We immediately slunk off into the long grass and bushes and under this cover climbed a ridge where I was able to survey the surrounding country with the aid of field glasses, yet no signs of life were visible. I was pretty sure, though, that the Germans would have an outpost lying somewhere near this cross-roads to give their main body warning and ambush our forces, which they must know would be coming along soon. I told two men to remain concealed on the ridge with old Brihemu and watch the three roads, while I with two others and the young native followed the other track for three or four miles. Still seeing neither sight nor sign of the enemy I tried to get into touch with other villagers, who might give us information about the body of men who had just passed ; but these parts were wild and almost uninhabited, so I made back to the men I had left behind and there was excitedly told the news that they had seen two soldiers leaving a clump of bush by the roadside to draw water at the small stream. This gave me some clue and it was not difficult to imagine where the German outpost was hiding.

Brihemu, one of the pluckiest old men for his age (about sixty), volunteered to crawl through the long grass to the next ridge where he hoped to get a full view of the enemy, explaining that he alone was less likely to be seen than if we all went. I agreed to this plan and the old man stealthily disappeared in the grass, returning in about an hour to say that he had seen the Germans, about thirty or forty in all, hiding where I suspected—by the roadside.

N

I knew what this meant—they were waiting to open fire on our advance guard or cut up lonely scouting parties, such as ourselves ; but this time they were caught at their little game, which they had played so often at our expense.

We returned to the main force and I reported to the Major, who told me I could have what men I liked to try and wipe out the outpost. I took only twenty good men, as we should have to do a great deal of hill climbing and I was afraid a larger force would be liable to become cumbersome. Before dawn my little party moved off and old Brihemu took us over some very rough country. By midday we had come out on the German road, but this time between them and their own line of retreat. I arranged my men in extended order and advanced towards the outpost.

Over the brow of the hill I caught sight of a sentry, so placed as to be quite hidden from the British side, but exposed to our present position. Then on looking closer I noticed in the long grass a row of askaris and a couple of white officers ready to receive our column, which they had evidently caught sight of in the distance.

We were only a hundred and fifty yards away now and the enemy quite unconscious of our presence, so intent were they watching. I ordered the men to open up a sudden fire. The Germans, evidently thinking a large force was upon them, stayed not a moment, but scuttled off into the long grass as fast as they could, and owing to the nature of the country most of them got away by going down into a deep bush-covered ravine.

We advanced cautiously up to the position and found we had killed one askari and then, following the direction the enemy had taken, we made prisoners of two other askaris—the one severely injured and the other with a slight flesh wound in the leg. We carried both of them back and dressed their wounds by the side of the stream.

One of my men happened to be an ex-German askari and of the same tribe as the prisoners, so I told him to give his countrymen food and drink and try and make them feel at home, as I wanted to question them presently. He must explain that we English were the black man's friend and only had a quarrel with his German masters.

I had sent a chit to Major James explaining the position and saying I would await him where I was. Then I settled down in the German officer's comfortable easy chair, made of bundles of grass tied together and piled up in the form of an arm-chair, and I found it a most luxurious seat. I ordered one of the men to boil the German kettle, for I noticed on a little table before me a tin of coffee and some sugar and thought the Major would be glad of a cup of coffee when he came along. Upon opening the departed officer's two boxes we found in the first his spare clothing and a few knicknacks and most welcome of all, several hundred good cigarettes. The other box contained foodstuffs, amongst them a great polony sausage, some small sausages, two loaves of brown bread and a tin of dripping. These I fell upon ravenously, having been so busy on this trip that I had had little time to have food cooked.

I told the Punjabi sergeant that he might have some of the cigarettes, which he modestly accepted, and I then offered him a lump of polony, which he looked at hungrily but politely refused, saying he was a Mahomedan and it was against his religion to eat pig meat. I told him I was sure the sausages were mostly beef, but he explained that it was against his faith even to eat beef or the flesh of any other animal, unless the throat had been cut by a believer of the Prophet.

"You people as soldiers are very difficult to please. My men eat whatever I eat, but you and the other Indians deserve something of the spoil also. It is not fair that we should have it all. You have taken an equal share in this capture, now look well and see if there is anything you would like amongst all this stuff."

The Sergeant refused to take anything from sheer modesty, but knowing that none of the Indians were well off for rations I made him take a small bag of wheat meal, which I knew would come in useful to make his flat cakes with. I also gave him a quantity of dried beans, a lump of brown sugar and half a loaf of bread.

I found a great contrast between these Indians of the fighting castes and the East African shop-keepers, who were the only natives of India I had come in contact with up to the present ; they could fight and moreover were gentlemen and men of honourable dispositions.

I had just finished a hearty meal and, leaning back on the comfortable seat, called for a piece of burning wood from the fire to light one of the

German officer's cigarettes, as we had no matches, and was feeling generally pleased with the world, when suddenly a shot rang out from the sentry just above. A second later there followed a regular fusillade and the bullets came hissing and zipping about us.

" What ever was happening ? Had the Germans returned ? "

Everyone was up in an instant and we arrived at the road to see the unfortunate Indian sentry lying in a pool of blood and just about gasping his last. All the men then started firing frantically at some fast-retiring figures amongst the trees. A return fire came for a short time—then all was silent and we went forward to find littered along the road half a dozen or so sacks of native meal, in fact provisions for a considerable force for several days.

A wounded porter was also lying amongst the jumble, from whom we learned that the party just encountered consisted of some forty askaris and two white men coming along to reinforce the picket. They had not noticed the difference in sentries until they had got right on top of the Punjabi and he immediately fired amongst them. The Germans then realizing that they had run into what might be a large force of British, returned a volley and took to their heels, the porters in their panic throwing away all their loads, as was generally the case in surprises like this.

When the boxes were wrenched open we found more foodstuffs, much as before, which of course could not have been more welcome. These Germans evidently were living like fighting cocks, while our transport could hardly bring in enough provisions to keep us alive.

Carefully wrapped up with sacking in one of the boxes I found the aluminium tail of one of our aerial bombs, bent and twisted from an explosion and evidently treasured by the German officer as a valuable souvenir.

Just as we had finished the examination, a young subaltern from the main body came up, bringing me orders to report to the Major, so I went back to find him camped by the stream near at hand. He congratulated me on the way I had dispersed the Germans, but my work was not yet done. He said that while the troops camped for the day, I must go forward and scout the country as far as the Ruvu River, about eight miles away, and try and get back again that evening, or early next morning, as the column would move forward shortly after dawn.

So I left with my four men and the two guides and we continued along the road for a mile or so ; but it was very ticklish work, for I knew that somewhere along that road would be lying the two parties of Germans we had just encountered and in no amiable frame of mind towards the men who had robbed them of their rations and other little comforts of life. On discussing the matter with Brihemu we decided that it would be much safer to make across country to the river. The old man led the way and after forcing our way through the long grass for some distance we came to a path leading to a little cluster of half a dozen huts, hidden away in the nook of the hill.

The father of the village came out and greeted Brihemu warmly. Apparently they were old cronies. The new-comer was a cheerful old soul and told us that he and one of his nephews had that very day been to the Ruvu River to catch fish and collect a certain herb which grows there and is a very good cure for swollen ankles, from which his wife was suffering. The old man then went on to explain that while he was talking to a friend at the village by the ford, a company of Germans with two white men crossed the river and camped there. The white men demanded eggs and told some of their men to catch the village chickens, while others ransacked the huts for grain. They were all seemingly very hungry and had no food of their own. The chief officer was in a great temper with his porters and declared he would have them all beaten when he got back to camp, and the poor porters looked much afraid and if they dared they would surely have run away. When he demanded tea to be made and learned that the cook had thrown his kettle and packets of tea away, he became more furious than ever, started cursing in his own language, and told the askaris to bring the unfortunate cook to him.

Old Brihemu chuckled away in enjoyment of the story as his friend continued excitedly :

" As the white man and the native sergeant were busy beating the cook, I took my little nephew by the hand and made off as quickly as we could go, for to tell the truth I was beginning to tremble with fear, so terrible was the wrath of that captain. But luck was against us, for the other white man saw me and sent one of the askaris to bring us back. I was afraid they were going to take me away to carry loads, which my poor old body could never stand, for you know Brihemu and I are old and I am not a well man any more. Then I remembered that the white man had lost all his loads and I plucked up courage and went forward with a lighter heart.

" ' What is that in your bundle ? '

" ' Only herbs for my poor old wife's leg.'   ·

" ' Open them and let me see.' (I did so displaying the stuff before the captain.) ' Oh, throw the things away. But, ach, there is another bundle. What is in that one ? '

" ' Fish ' (said I).

" ' Yes, they will do nicely with the fowl. Cook, get up from the ground and clean them at once, instead of lying there as if you were truly hurt. But, old man, why were you trying to slink off ? Were you taking a message to those *schwein Englanders* ? '

" ' No,' said I humbly, ' the English are no friends of mine.' "

" ' Have you any native tobacco in your village ? I hear that tobacco grows well in this part of the Ruvu and those English have taken all my Tabora cigarettes.'

" Although I had much cured tobacco in my hut I said to the officer that I had none, not wanting his askaris to come poking about my village. At this the captain again cursed in his own language, asked the other white man if he had any cigarettes, and when he heard that he had not, all his anger returned, and he told an askari to give me five lashes with a *keboko*, just to hurry me on, as he said. Fortunately they were not very severe ones and they certainly did help me along, for I did not stop until I arrived here," concluded the old man with a grin.

While I was questioning other natives about the surrounding country and busy making a sketch map from what they told me, assisted by the little I had seen, I noticed Brihemu and his old friend going off, deeply engrossed in some earnest conversation with much nodding of the grey old heads and gestures with skinny old hands.   A little later Brihemu came back and said his friend had told him of a small German picket on the road.   One of his young men had seen it from a hill-top only that morning and it had been stationed there for over a week.   Mounting the hill behind the village the young man pointed out to me the exact spot in the far distance.   I then continued my way to the Ruvu, as my orders were to go as far as the river, and then hurried back to the main body arriving there about ten p.m.   At first I decided to lie outside the British pickets until dawn and so settled down in the long grass to get some rest, but whenever I closed my eyes I thought of that big German sausage and the loaf of bread and dripping in the box, luxuries which we had not tasted for months, and the more I thought about them the hungrier I seemed to get.   The night was chilly and I had no blanket, but at last I fell into a wakeful sleep, only to dream of the polony in the box.

I dreamed that we were fighting terrible battles

with the German captain and his askaris, who had
come back for their polony. Men were shooting
each other down wholesale, but they stood up again
as fast as they went down, so the polony remained
safely in its box. Then our Major ordered a
bayonet charge, and I charged along with bushy
bearded Punjabis, who with fierce war cries, spiked
Germans on the end of their bayonets, until I
remember coming face to face with the German
captain. The only weapon I seemed to have in
my hand was a bayonet fastened at the end of a
stick with string, and whenever I tried to kill
anyone the bayonet bent over. Meanwhile the
German officer had drawn a long shining sword
and was slowly pushing it inch by inch into my
body. Then as the battle for the polony was
raging at its highest I saw old Brihemu standing
on a precipice overlooking the fighting hosts, and
with a huge watering can, in which he loudly
announced was Ruvu water, he sprinkled the
opposing armies and as the water descended upon
them their rifles, which were now red hot, hissed
and let off steam.

Vapour arose, the armies disappeared and I
found myself lying in the grass with a hard pebble
in my side. The night was pitch black and a cold
drizzle came down upon our faces.

The rain had also awakened my four men lying
nearby, and I could hear them talking together in
low whispers, as their teeth chattered with the cold ;
for we had left our overcoats behind to enable us to
march with greater ease. Then the whole night
was filled with a deep-noted roar, followed by

several " grunt-grunts " which resounded and echoed up and down the numerous ravines.

" *Simba !* " (lion) whispered one of the voices at my side, and everyone stopped to listen, letting the King of Beasts have full monopoly of the night ; but the sound stopped as suddenly as it had begun, and for half an hour we sat in dead silence. Then it again commenced this time farther down the valley.

" The lion is after the Indians," said my Corporal to the others, and I thought I heard a little chuckle.

Hardly had the Corporal said the words when three sudden flashes flared out on the next ridge, and this time the echoes of the still night were wakened by the report of three rifles, which must have scared off the lions, for we heard no more of them.

I again thought of the German sausage and all the other good things in the box, also my warm blankets, so I told the Corporal that now we knew where one of the pickets was, we would attempt to get into the camp. Stumbling along through the darkness we got up as near to the picket as we thought safe. A horrid sensation is this, creeping up even to one's own pickets at night, when every moment you expect the blinding flash of a rifle in your face ; for on these occasions, sentries are inclined to shoot first and challenge afterwards.

Everything was dead silent, although I knew the picket must have heard us stumbling over the loose stones of the hill-side. We stopped and I holler'd out in English, but received no reply. So I called out again. My voice seemed so loud in the night that I feared it would awaken the whole British camp, only about half a mile beyond ; but still there was no reply. Yet I thought I heard Indian voices carrying on an argument in low, excited tones. Then realizing how far sounds carry in the stillness of the night, I addressed the picket in my ordinary speaking voice. This time there came a reply.

" Is that you, Intelligence Sahib ? "

" Yes."

" Come on, we will not shoot."

You can imagine my joy when I heard the voice of the old Sergeant who had been with me and with whom I had become quite friends. Soon I was sitting down with the Indian picket of four, carrying on a whispered conversation with the Sergeant.

" We thought you were a ghost lion and trying to betray us into letting ourselves be caught."

" A ghost lion ? " said I, a little puzzled.

" Yes, in India we all know that there are ghost tigers, so in Africa there must be ghost lions. These animals in India are bad people who have become tigers. They can talk and sing just like us, and in a jungle near my home young men have been enticed away by the singing and laughter of what they thought a beautiful maiden, but when they got to the place there was the big ghost tigress waiting to eat them up."

The Sergeant, whilst speaking, put a plate containing curried beans and delightful flat cakes before me saying :—

" Eat, Intelligence Sahib, for you have done

much walking to-day and let us not speak about the ghost lions and tigers any more."

It ended by our sleeping the night with the picket, for the Indians, who had their greatcoats as well as blankets, were able to lend us some covering. The arrangement, I think, suited both parties equally well, because we did not like the idea of blundering into the camp at dead of night, and the Indians were glad of our company, the thought of ghost lions and the roar of real ones being still fresh in their memories. They seemed to think that my Africans had some method of charming these creatures.

Early next morning I reported to the Major and we moved on towards the Ruvu, and at a certain place picked up old Brihemu, who had remained at his friend's house for the night. I guided the troops along the same path we had travelled the day before, not wanting to disturb the German picket on the main road as I had at the back of my mind a plan for dealing with them later.

We camped on a little hill overlooking the broad sandy bed of the Ruvu River, and I laid my plans before the Major, who gave me sixty men, a machine-gun and an Indian Lieutenant, the only native in the Regiment who could speak English. I think this must have been one of the very few cases in this campaign where a white N.C.O. was placed in charge over the head of an Indian Lieutenant.

I told fifteen men under my friend the Sergeant go to back along the path with old Brihemu until he struck the main road, then advance along it in extended order, as if they were the advance guard of a large column. When they were within rifle range of the enemy's position they were to open up a fusillade and thus cause the picket to retire. Meanwhile I, with the fifty men and a machine-gun, would be waiting at the ford, where the Germans must cross the river to get to their main body.

When we arrived at the ford I found it was an ideal place for an ambush. The sandy bed of the river was about fifty yards broad and along our bank was a fringe of tall bushes and grass, behind which I lined the men, and as I did so I felt that if the enemy came along that path nothing on earth could save them from being cut up. The thing which worried me, however, was that the river at this time of the year was only about a foot deep and there was nothing to prevent the Germans from crossing at any other place. So I sent two sergeants, each with a dozen men, to patrol the river banks to right and left and should they see any likely-looking crossing they were to hide there and watch it.

I had heard the men along the road firing at the picket some twenty minutes ago, so by this time the enemy should be hurrying towards me. Then, to our great excitement, the German's baggage came in sight, five porters with loads and the cook. These men were hurriedly and noiselessly seized as they clambered up the bank beyond the fringe of rushes and long grass. Everyone's eyes were now glued to the opening on the far bank, while the hands of the man behind the machine-gun, I noticed, twitched with anticipation.

The minutes passed, but nothing stirred, so I asked one of the prisoners if their master was following by that road and he assured us quite genuinely that he was ; but the Germans it turned out, had sent their baggage along the main road and taken a short cut themselves. Suddenly firing broke out a little way downstream and I took half the men and hurried in that direction, but was very much disappointed to find that the enemy's party had got away into the long grass. One of their number, however, had been wounded and was brought in later by some of the local natives.

Although this little enterprise of ours had failed, owing to the unexpected movement of the Germans, I felt that this sort of thing was bound to do a lot morally for our good, as I had noticed the enemy generally had been getting into the way of expecting our advancing columns to attack from the front, where they of course had prepared a position, and would often wait until the very last moment before retiring and thus be able to do a lot more damage to the advance guard than if they had to contend with the possibility of an ambush party getting between them and their line of retreat. In this way we could give the enemy's advance posts a pretty thin time, for we British undoubtedly had an advantage over them in having the sympathies of the local natives on our side, though this valuable asset was only too often abused through the sheer ignorance and pig-headedness of troops from overseas. However, in my present case I had the good fortune of being attached to a regiment whose commander and second-in-command had the

common   sense   to   understand   the   value   of
the assistance of the local natives.

The next day we joined up with the Colonel of the
Punjabis, with the remainder of the regiment and
two batteries of mountain guns, which were carried
in sections on the backs of mules and manned by
Indian gunners.   That afternoon I found fresh
guides who would take us to Tulo, on the way
surprising two small parties of Germans, from one
of which we captured the white N.C.O. in charge.

On nearing Tulo I was informed by the inhabitants that the position was already in the hands of
the British forces which had advanced from the
other side.   There had not been a battle at the
place, for the Germans, destroying everything they
could not carry away, had retired to a position on
the Mgeta River, where they dug themselves in on
the one bank while our forces dug themselves in
on the other and trench warfare prevailed for
several months.

CHAPTER XXIII

BIG GAME AND A CAPTURE

GENERAL Headquarters remained at Tulo, so we I.D. men were also stationed there. Although the two armies were now comparatively at rest, only snarling at each other across the river, like two dogs still angry, but too weary to fight, we were kept continuously active, ever on the watch and spying out some new movements on the flanks.

I again met several of my old scout companions at Tulo and, Lewis coming up, I joined forces with him once more and at different times we went out on scouting expeditions as far as Lake Nserekera and the Rufiji. The country around these parts, especially that broad stretch of uninhabited land between the Mgeta and the Rufiji, might be termed one of the finest sportsman's paradises in all the parts we had passed through. On making a trip down to Lake Nserekera we saw many kinds of game all in one day. We left camp early and hardly had we got clear of the outskirts when we came upon a pack of twenty wild dogs running down an unfortunate doe reedbuck. A little later on we saw two small herds of giraffe, while every half-mile or so, looking through the open bush which grew all around, we could see groups of antelope peacefully grazing or regarding us with curiosity as we went by. Then on coming to the Mgeta River, at a place near its entrance to the Ruvu, we were told by a native that there was a crocodile at the ferry where the women drew water and it often waited there in hopes of catching one of them. I looked over the low banks and sure enough there was the monster's nose just visible above the muddy water. Not wanting to give our position away to the enemy by a shot, we scared the reptile off by throwing stones at it. Lewis and I, entering a dug-out canoe, crossed the narrow but swift-flowing channel, and then the canoe went back for the men. Four of them entered and came across safely, and the canoe returned for the third time. Now there were six men left and they all scrambled into the frail craft which, in the middle of the stream, suddenly turned on its side and sank. The Corporal, being of the Kavirondo tribe, swam out easily, bringing his rifle and equipment safely with him ; but the rest of the poor fellows, who were natives from the highlands of East Africa, could not swim a stroke and all clung desperately to each other in a tight knot, which bobbed up and down and occasionally dipped below the surface as it floated down-stream. Things looked pretty desperate for the four men— the river was deep and we knew that there was at least one large man-eating crocodile lurking not far off. Lewis and I hardly knew what to do, so suddenly had the thing happened, and it seemed almost impossible to save the men from their fate, when two of the local natives standing nearby without a word leapt headlong into the water.

They were splendid swimmers and we saw them cautiously approach the cluster of drowning men and slowly draw them towards a sandbank near the edge of the river, where they were able to find their feet. By this time somebody had brought a rope and the rescued men were hauled up the bank, some of them almost unconscious, but still grasping tenaciously to each other. The rifles had been lost at the bottom of the river, with the exception of one which had got tightly jammed between the cluster of men. Hardly had the last man been hoisted clear of the water when shouts of " Crocodile ! " were heard and a snout and two wicked-looking eyes appeared and looked up at us insolently not ten yards away. The sharp-eared monster had evidently heard the commotion in the water from somewhere down-stream and hurried to the sound, only to find that he was half a minute too late. So insolently did he regard us, with a look of sullen disappointment, as one who had been wrongfully robbed of his rights, sending a shudder of horror through the men who had just been rescued, and so filled was I with disgust and repugnance that I determined to put an end to the brute, even if the shot were to give our position away. We were, after all, not near to any of the enemy's outposts and the danger was not very great, so I took steady aim and placed a bullet between its two projecting eyes. The water was churned to foam as the huge scaly brute turned frenzied somersaults. Then a pair of great open jaws and two thick waving arms and wicked claws appeared above the bloodstained water as the crocodile leapt upwards and fell back lifeless, showing a great slimy, yellowish green belly, which soon sank below the surface and was swept away by the current.

Next my attention was turned to the two villagers who had acted so boldly, and Lewis and I, discussing the matter, decided to give the men the money which had been issued to us for secret service expenses and which we were allowed to use at our own discretion—about fifty rupees. The natives were highly delighted and the elder of the two said he would rescue our rifles as well. With that he sent the younger man to his village near at hand, and in a quarter of an hour half a dozen men appeared armed with spears and stabbing knives. They threw off their loin clothes and dived into the river, and in spite of the strong current and deep water and probability of more crocodiles, brought up all the rifles in a very short space of time. The canoe also was dragged from the bottom of the river.

We then went on our way, soon leaving all traces of human habitation behind and often seeing game of various kinds. A few hours later we found ourselves right amongst a herd of about fifty elephants. The grass and bushes were thick and it was difficult work picking a way through the great sleeping bulks. Fortunately some of our men, as well as myself, had had previous experience of the ways of these animals and the elephants in these parts had evidently not often been fired upon, and were very placid ; so we got the men through without having to fire a single shot, which was fortunate, as any sudden disturbance might have stampeded the herd upon us. A little farther on we came upon a sleeping rhino who went off like a snorting locomotive engine. Just as we were having our midday meal another herd of elephants walked by, only about a hundred yards away ; but we kept perfectly quiet and they took not the slightest notice of us. At one of the numerous rain pools I studied the spoor and found that lion and buffalo were also plentiful in this wonderful piece of game country. On a previous trip we had almost walked right into two buffaloes in comparatively open country. They wheeled round as if to charge, but thinking better of it galloped away into the cover of some long grass. Giraffe could also occasionally be seen lumbering along with their awkward strides or peacefully browsing off the tree-tops. In fact, I have never seen such a hunter's paradise as this, especially as it was when our troops first arrived there ; but war soon took its toll of the game. Near Tulo camp animals were shot at ruthlessly, often by men in search of meat, but only too frequently by little parties out to amuse themselves. I have seen great beautiful giraffe shot down by soldiers out for a walk, just for the few hairs in its tail which were used for making souvenir bracelets. When eventually the front lines moved forward, our lines of communication, I believe, slaughtered elephants wholesale, until proper administration was established.

One night on the Mgeta River two elephants walked calmly along no-man's-land between the two entrenched forces, and each side thought that the monsters were some new form of tank or other modern implement of destruction about to charge down upon them. So they let off such a hail of lead, both from machine-guns and rifles, that the unfortunate animals' legs were literally cut from beneath them and their bodies punctured as leaky as sieves, and there they lay for weeks to decompose, neither side daring to go out and claim the tusks.

Whilst stationed at Tulo we had the good fortune of serving for part of the time under a chief who was not merely content with sitting and directing from H.Q., but was one who believed in seeing things for himself. We had heard of Captain La Fontaine before, for as a lieutenant he made a remarkable reconnaisance patrol from Kahi to ascertain the existence of the Handeni Mombo tram line, and hardly had he been in charge at Tulo a week when he expressed a desire to accompany us to Lake Nserekera, near the Rufiji. We took with us a force of some twenty askaris and marched that morning as far as the Mgeta River, crossed in the afternoon and marched on until midnight, camping in the middle of the waterless belt on the way to the Rufiji. We saw several herds of elephant, but nothing of the enemy until the third day, when we were on our return journey and quite close to our own camp. Here we came upon a small party of two Germans, whites, and half a dozen askaris. As we were coming from the direction of their own camp they mistook us for Germans, but must have been a little doubtful, for they stopped and sent one of their askaris on ahead to meet us. Captain La Fontaine, after having the man's rifle and ammunition removed, told him to go back and tell his Bwana to surrender. The Germans, however, had been observing us through their field-glasses and thought it was time they made their escape, so moved off ; but unfortunately for them there was open country beyond them and we gave chase, letting off shots as we hurried along. We eventually began to overtake them, and in any case they had little chance of escape because there was no alternative for them but to make straight for our own camp, as our little force, now well extended, cut them off from any other retreat. The two white men were soon run to a standstill and throwing away their rifles and equipment, held up a white handkerchief in surrender. Our askaris were, however, thoroughly " worked up " over the chase and turned a deaf ear to the order to cease fire, and the O.C., Lewis and myself, as well as the native sergeant, had literally to beat the men back to prevent them from murdering the Germans in cold blood. As it was our native sergeant's gun went off as he struck one of the men with the muzzle and the poor fellow was shot through the body, dying almost instantaneously. The only thing which saved the two Germans was that our men were so puffed and shaky with the long run that none of them seemed able to shoot straight.

When order was restored the Germans must have thought that if they handed over their valuables the askaris might not again be tempted to take their lives, or something of this sort, for suddenly both of them produced a watch, the one a valuable gold one and the other the largest silver watch I have ever seen, as well as a small collection of coins which they pressed me to take. I don't know why they picked upon me out of the three of us, but they seemed quite determined that I should have their valuables. The O.C. told them we did not want their personal belongings, and he would see that they were safe in their own possession, whereupon they reluctantly returned their watches to their pockets. One of the Germans was quite a good catch, as he knew this part of the country well and was responsible, we believed, for land mines placed on the main road some little time previously.

CHAPTER XXIV

MEASLES AND MANGOES

THE brigade to which I was attached was ordered to proceed to Kilwa, a port on the east coast which had recently been taken by the naval forces. This meant a journey first to the Central Railway, where we would take train to Dar-es-Salaam, and travel from there to our destination by boat. I had not seen civilization for about a year and a half. It had been almost continual march, march, march, either on starvation rations or sometimes none at all, so I was greatly excited, as were many others, at the prospect of getting back to a civilized seaport town, where everyone was living on the fat of the land. We expected to stay some days in Dar-es-Salaam, waiting for the boat, and my pals and I were long speculating and discussing what we would do when we first got into the capital.

We had now been marching some days, the next day we would reach the railway and then it would only take a day by rail to the fair city of plenty ; but my luck was against me. I had had a terrible headache all day and took quinine for fever, but felt no better. That evening I had a temperature and became covered in red spots and I was carried from Dar-es-Salaam station on a stretcher off to hospital, suffering from measles ! Yes, measles of all things, which I thought I had done with years ago as a kid ! But measles they declared I had and into hospital I had to go and, worse still, into an isolation tent all by myself, where I seemed to be just left and entirely forgotten for a time. However, after the temperature had gone down, food was brought to me, but not half enough. The hospital attendant seemed to forget that I had been starving for over a year. Two days later I meekly and rather nervously said I wanted some more food, but was looked upon so fiercely by the great fat lump of an orderly that I never had the courage to ask again.

Even when I was over the fever stages of my illness I was not allowed to go out of the tent, but by pulling over the back flap I could look out on to the road, and for hours I would sit watching the passers-by. One day, to my surprise, I saw my old pal Duirs go past, and he, too, was in hospital garb.

" Hullo, Eddie ! " I called out. He stopped short and looked around to see where the sound came from until I called again and he walked round to the door of the tent.

" Come inside quickly," I said, " for if some of these conscripts and conscientious objectors, who call themselves hospital orderlies, see us, they will pretty soon see you off. I am supposed to be in the isolation ward, but I don't see why they should keep me in close confinement now the measles are over. It is good to talk to a human being again. How do they feed you in the big hospital ? "

" Oh, rotten ! " said Eddie, " The food is good

enough—all sorts of fancy stuff, but not half enough of it."

" Have you noticed what a lot of fine mangoes there are about this place ? I have seen natives going backwards and forwards with baskets full on their heads, apparently for sale, Why not let us buy a basketful and hide it in this tent ? Then you can always come down here to my tent for a feed."

" Not in these trousers ! " said Eddie, looking down at his hospital flannels, which were so large that they had to be turned up about a foot at the ends. " If I were to put my nose outside the hospital bounds in this uniform the Red Caps would have me in no time. It is a crime, you know, to eat anything out of hospital, or bring food in. Too many dysentery and enteric cases have been killed, I believe in this way. "

" Oh ! " said I, a little downhearted, and we both lapsed into a gloomy silence, I thinking of the ripe mangoes the while.

Duirs then told me an amusing story of how two fellows in the next beds to him sneaked up town in their hospital clothes, but got caught by Red Caps who were watching out for them. It seemed more difficult, I thought, to get up town than we had found it to get behind the German lines. There was one thing about being out at the front—we could scrounge around for something to eat, even if we did not get much rations.

Then a sudden idea came to me and I said :—

" I suppose they pinched all your clothes when they dished you out those grey things ? "

" Yes, everything except my shorts and puttees. I thought of that, but it is no use, one could not go up town without a shirt on."

" But wait a minute, I had two shirts and hid one because it had some papers in the pockets which I did not want them to get hold of. Now go and fetch your things and we can take turn about with the complete rig-out."

Duirs soon returned with the puttees and shorts safely hidden under his long coat—the hospital staff were much too busy to watch us closely—and soon I went striding down the street in a complete uniform—khaki flannel shirt rolled up at the sleeves, khaki drill shorts, puttees and my boots (which fortunately they had left me). The fact that I had no socks inside the boots, nor vest below the rough shirt, which was scraping my skin, made no difference to the military police post, whom I strode past, to all outward appearance dressed exactly like the hundreds of other soldiers wandering about the streets.

The first place I went to was the National Bank of India, who fortunately had just opened a branch in the conquered town. Then, with money in my pocket, I went to a Greek teashop and had a real blow out of tea and cakes. Afterwards, passing a native with a large basket of ripe mangoes, I purchased the lot for a rupee, as mangoes were very plentiful on this coast. I had the fruit put in a sack and in this way eventually safely smuggled them into the tent. Duirs, who had been anxiously watching operations from a top-story window, soon came along and we sat on our haunches in that isolation tent with the sack of mangoes between us and ate and ate, as we hardly believed it possible to eat. We both seemed to have a craving for fruit and other sweet things, I suppose having existed so long without them. For some unknown reason the doctors in hospital denied mangoes even to convalescents, saying they were not good for invalids ; but we thrived and grew fat on them, consuming large quantities each day, which either Duirs or I took it in turns to bring back after little outings.

We remained on in hospital as convalescents for another week, and I shall never forget the wonderful sea bathing we used to get every afternoon on the beach just opposite our hospital, which in peace time had been a German hotel. Within our bounds there was a long sandy beach where the men could cast off their clothes and go into the clear blue water, which was so warm that it was possible to stay in for hours. Duirs and I would sometimes swim out into deep water and take command of a dinghy which we found tied to a buoy some distance from the shore. The dinghy belonged to a tug which worked in the harbour all day, so we used to unfasten it and amuse ourselves by rowing about the bay or catching fish. One day, however, the crew of the tug had a half-holiday, and when they tied up at their buoy they discovered there was no dinghy to take them on shore and so they proceeded to hunt us up in the tug. We saw it coming and rowed for dear life towards the shallows, where we knew our pursuers could not follow, but the tug was too fast for us and as we saw we were about to be caught we threw away the oars and swam for the shore. It was sometime before the sailors could collect their oars and board the dingy to give chase and by the time they reached the beach we had hurried into our clothes and were well out of sight.

So well had we been thriving on our extra diet of mangoes that we got better twice as quickly as any of the other patients and the next day were discharged from the hospital. On reporting at our Headquarters I was ordered to proceed to Kilwa and Duirs to Lindi, two ports fairly recently occupied by our troops and from which invading forces were being pushed inland ; but it would be a week or ten days before our boat was ready to sail, so we had time to kill in the most interesting town, which was now British Headquarters for all East African operations.

Both Duirs and I had lost that keenness of appetite which we had at first experienced and we once more became normal beings, able to pass a basket of ripe mangoes or a Greek teashop without turning a hair. We spent the time as everyone seemed to do here, lazily lying or hovering about. In the morning we used to bathe at the beach near our camp, but for the afternoon bathe we found a most excellent place just beyond the narrow entrance of the mouth of the harbour. At low tide the water would roll back leaving sparkling sands for nearly a mile which would lie and bake in the sunshine all day and in the afternoon the clear blue water would come rippling back again over the hot beach. Thus when we came down to bathe

the water would be about five feet deep and it was like swimming in a huge warm bath. It was so delightful that we often stayed there until after dark, swimming sometimes nearly a mile out over this shallow sand bed, then walking back to camp through the night.

Other things of interest were the two German wrecks, both of which we explored. The one was a large ocean liner, sunk by our naval guns under aeroplane direction while the boat lay anchored and safe, as the enemy thought, hidden from view of the ocean by tall palms growing on the beach. For months now it had been lying on its side in comparatively shallow water and was almost submerged at high tide.

The other wreck, a cargo steamer, had been intended by our enemies to block up the narrow entrance of the bay. A great floating dry-dock had first been sunk right in the narrow channel and then this boat was hauled in place to complete the blockade ; but for some unknown reason our enemies tried to do their work of mischief while the tidal current was running strong, given greater force by the narrowness of the channel, and the boat was swept out of place. Then the British guns out at sea opened fire and the Germans allowed the doomed craft to drift. She was swept towards the land and by this time, receiving several direct hits in the bows, she grounded and then lay on her side, only a few yards from the shore, while the entrance for our shipping lay open, and the Germans were powerless to do any more harm as they were soon driven out of the town.

Duirs and I, having stripped off our clothes, swam out and soon reached the slanting wall of the wrecked steamer and walked over the deserted deck, which was tilted at an angle of 45°. Everything of any use had been stripped by the bluejackets or other sailors in the harbour. Having gone down the ladderway we explored until we came to the water level and there watched multicoloured fish which had swum in from the ocean and were using the hold as their playground.

We were making our way home when something dark lying in the sand attracted our attention, and going up to it we found an unexploded twelve-inch naval shell, which months back had evidently been fired at the boat we had just left. It was about four or five feet long and so heavy and solid that we could not move it—indeed, it would have taken at least six or eight men to lift it. I could not help wondering at the colossal force which had been placed behind that missile to hurl it from the cruiser far out at sea to this point. Yet this gigantic shell was not the largest of its kind, for one heard our naval men sitting in the Greek teashops talking in quite a casual way of their eighteen and sixteen inches.

The next day I walked down town to say goodbye to some fellows I knew in hospital, for my boat was leaving on the morrow. I took the short cut from our camp to the hospital, which was across the bay by boat, passing several ocean liners and steamers riding at anchor. Most of the boats had been in harbour when I arrived and were still lying there, I suppose they found the " Haven

DESTROYED BRIDGE ON RAILWAY

[p. 188.

THE BRITISH SET THE DAMAGED RAILWAY RUNNING

[p. 190.

FOR WEEKS WE DID CONSTANT PATROLLING

[p. 64.

of Rest " (which is the meaning of Dar-es-Salaam)
so pleasant that they could not tear themselves
away to brave the dangers of the high seas.   At
Dar-es-Salaam certainly nobody was making much
of a hustle to win the war.

I gave the ferry boy a half-rupee and climbed on
to a little landing and was soon in the town, which
seemed as crowded as ever.   The number of officers
one saw was remarkable in proportion to the men,
and many of them seemed to have military cars or
motor bikes, while our transport at the front was
mighty short of vehicles at this time.   The first day
I set eyes on the place I was astounded as to what
they could all be doing.   There seemed more able-
bodied men in khaki pottering about here at the
base, I suppose organizing our rations, than there
were fighting at the front.   Yet still we seemed to
get very little to eat in the firing line.

As I walked along one of the main streets my
attention was attracted by a spruce figure leisurely
peddling a very bumpy solid-tyred bicycle along the
street.

" Hullo ! " said I.   " Whatever are you doing
here, riding about on that thing ? "

The man came to a halt, for he was one of the
old E.A.M.R., and we had done many a picket and
patrol together.

" Oh, I have got a staff job and am stationed here
at Headquarters, and a damned fine place it is, too.
None of your shortage of rations and forced marches!
Here, we have tons of amusements in the evenings—
plays and cinemas—and a cushy job in the daytime.
I got a pal I knew at college to wangle it for me.

P

He is a captain, so we don't know each other, of course, when we pass in the street."

I eyed my old companion, then his bicycle, and said, rather mystified, " But what is your job ? "

" Well," said he, " my job, you know, is carrying important documents from our office to Headquarters to be signed and countersigned. But I only work in the mornings. Before taking up the job I got my O.C. pal to promise that I could have the afternoons off, so he has a native boy to take them in the afternoon."

" You are doing the work of a messenger boy, then," I said a little disdainfully. " What a come down ! "

" I should not put it quite like that," he protested. " You would not get your rations at the front, or any kit or ammunition, if those letters were not signed, and some of them are most important too." And with that he nodded a good humoured farewell and slowly peddled off, humming a merry little tune as he went along.

CHAPTER XXV

BACK TO WORK IN EARNEST

THAT evening I went on board and in due course arrived at Kilwa Kisiwani, a place some sixteen miles from the old seaport town of Kilwa which was too shallow for steamboats. We landed by means of a row-boat on to a makeshift landing-stage, for Kisiwani, before the British landed, had not been used as a port, though there was an excellent bay of deep water. An hour's run along the coast in a motor lorry brought us to the ancient Arabic town of Kilwa Kivinje, which was now British Headquarters and all buildings previously occupied by the Germans had been taken over by our forces. I found Intelligence Headquarters installed in a cool white building and was told that I would have to remain in the town for a few days before being attached to a company of Indian troops, who were going out to the front, which was now at Kibata, some sixty miles inland, where considerable activities were taking place.

I was found comfortable quarters and after settling in took a look around. All the buildings as well as the narrow streets were glaring white and the houses mostly of Arabic design. Along the old and crumbling sea wall just in front of my quarters was a row of very ancient and rusty muzzle-loader cannons of antique pattern, now long since fallen into disuse, but at one time playing an important part by commanding the water of the shallows just below them. When I first saw the bay the tide was out and there on the dry sand lay two Arabic dhows from which walked a string of porters chanting their song as they unloaded the cargo and carried it to the shore. It appears that an ideal Arabic port, unlike ours, is one in which the water is shallow enough to run the vessels aground, where loading and unloading can be done at low tide. On going some distance along the bay, which was now nothing but a flat sandy bed, I came to the native fisheries which supply the town with that valuable commodity. The fishing is also done by means of the tide, a tall fence of thin sticks stuck well into the ground and fastened securely together with cross-pieces runs for half a mile or so along the beach, curving inwards at each extreme end. As the tide comes in the water surface rises well over the fence and fish in search of food swim over the top or around the sides. So busy are they feeding that they do not attempt to get back to deep water before the tide is half out, when they find it too late, as the fence bars their escape, so the fishermen have nothing more to do than gather them into their baskets. The day that I arrived on the scene the tide had just gone out, but the catch was a very poor one and the owner of the trap, a cheerful Swahili not overburdened with work, seemed inclined to chat freely and told me that on occasions he caught very large fish, even full-grown sharks, which the town folks relished and which he cut up and sold by the pound.

The next day I explored the town which consisted of the usual narrow streets of these coastal ports, with rows of little Indian or Arabic shops on either side, not much larger than stalls, where the owners sat crosslegged amongst their wares. I walked some miles out of town and the country all around was covered with beautiful shady mango trees, with ripe fruit hanging ready to be picked. Such was the outward appearance of Kilwa Kivinje, but under the shade of these same trees and in every dark corner of those white buildings lurked the deadly malaria mosquitoes. Even the feet of the common house fly were covered with the microscopic dysentery germs and already the hospital was full to overflowing with malaria and dysentery cases, yet more and more pouring in from the front, wasted with disease.

The next day I was told by Headquarters that the troops I was to be attached to would be a few days late and owing to sickness the Intelligence staff was very short-handed at the front, so I must proceed forward at once. I learned that some mule wagons were going out that very day, so I packed my few belongings, hurried to the transport lines and just caught the last wagon.

After about six or seven miles travel we left the pleasant mango and coco-nut trees of the coastal belt and again I was in the familiar bush-covered country. Our roads winding through low bush were highly scented here and there by a decayed mule or donkey, for in these parts there was pestilence amongst beasts as well as men, and transport animals were only able to do about a month or six weeks work, when they were just unharnessed by the Cape boy drivers and left by the roadside to die.

I joined up with Lewis at Chemera and we both pushed on towards the front, where heavy fighting had just taken place at Kibata. As we neared the camp we again heard the boom of more German 4.1 naval guns. Our orders were to report at General Headquarters at a place known as the Mission, as there were several large deserted mission houses and a church there, now being used as a field hospital and General Headquarters.

The nature of the country in these parts was rolling hills covered in the usual bush. There was no running water or open springs and all the drinking water for the army was drawn from a few dirty wells. However, fresh ones were being dug when we arrived, as it had been discovered that water could be found a few feet below the ground almost everywhere in the valley.

Lewis and I were soon back at our old job of scouting [and reconnoitring the enemy. The natives in these parts, though very friendly towards the British, were not quite so reliable, we found, as those encountered before, often fearing to give information of the German outposts, just because they would have the dangerous task of guiding us to the spot. Thus at first it was often very difficult to know if information received was correct and this all tended to make our work more difficult and dangerous and when any very important information was required we, if possible, obtained it from two or more entirely different sources, and even then sifted and analysed it before feeling justified in sending in a report to Headquarters for them to work upon.

At this time we, with a force of twenty askaris, had our Headquarters concealed on a bush-covered hill at Nyandete, about six miles away from the Mission, our G.H.Q., and only two miles from the nearest enemy post at Limbanguku. We were at first fairly safe, as they did not know the where-abouts of our hiding-place, but about a week after-wards, through some captured natives, the Germans found out the extreme weakness of our outpost and with threats of death made one of the captured men guide them to our hiding-place. At the grey of dawn they rushed the camp with an overwhelming force; but, as luck would have it, Lewis and I, with all the men except three, were out on a recon-noitring patrol. However, soon after this the Germans again made it pretty hot for us and we had to keep on the alert day and night for a sur-prise, besides doing our other Intelligence work.

To add to our discomfort, we were both suffering terribly from fever and dysentery and at last Lewis had to be sent back to Kilwa hospital. From there he eventually went on sick leave to his home in Australia and I was left to carry on alone once more. I, too, would have just loved to give up the struggle, for it seemed impossible to shake off the illness under these strenuous conditions; but now that I was the only Intelligence agent here, how could I go to hospital? Two other agents, I was told, were being sent up, but the one got ill on the way and the other went on the sick list two days after arrival.

The Germans had made another attempt at wiping up my camp, but I got to hear about it just in the nick of time and when they found they were being watched they returned, without doing any damage. But the illness and constant strain were beginning to prey on my nerves, so I asked my O.C. if I might move my camp two miles nearer to the main body, seeing I had been found out by the enemy. But all my troubles seemed to come at once, for on top of everything else I had a somewhat eccentric O.C. and on this occasion he wrote me a long letter, stressing the importance of holding Nyandete water-hole at all costs, as it was the very key to the German attack on the British flank. I might here mention that our O.C. was not one of the old I.D. officers, and I do not think he realized what he was asking me to do, possibly never having been out on an I.D. patrol himself.

So many of my native askaris became ill from dysentery and the constant tension we were living under that within a fortnight I had to send them all back, except six men. I myself was feeling much better again and for a month I lived the life of a bush ranger around Nyandete water-hole, never having a fixed camp but moving my position and sleeping in a fresh patch of scrub every night, and in this way I was able not only to watch the neighbourhood of the water-hole but also to safeguard myself to a certain extent, finding it far easier and less dangerous with six men than twenty. One day

I received an urgent message to leave my outpost temporarily and come in to the Mission. When I arrived at Headquarters my O.C. told me to reconnoitre towards the enemy's outpost, right in front of the main army and in an area which I had not worked on before, where almost every hill hid either the enemy's or our own outposts.

After getting in touch with the enemy, by way of a return journey, I was to advance on to one of our own outposts on the top of a hill in No-man's-land, half-way between the main body and the German's. I did as instructed and on ascending the hill was met by a terrific fusillade of machine-gun and rifle fire. I and most of my men got away into cover, of which fortunately there was plenty, but my party was scattered in every direction. We all naturally thought the enemy had taken the outpost, but you can imagine my disgust when, on returning to Headquarters, I learned that it was a British outpost after all which had fired upon us. They had not been warned by telephone of my movement, as arranged, and seeing us approaching them directly from the enemy's lines they naturally let us have it. Fortunately some of my men got left behind in hiding-places and, on seeing British troops, emerged and were able to explain the situation and bring back my personal effects, which the porters had thrown away.

The next day I went back to Nyandete, but for a fortnight we saw nothing of the Germans. I think they had given up the idea of ever catching my party. Also my position was now much improved, for I had gradually got the entire confidence of the local natives and established a system by which I was pretty well informed of all movements. Perhaps on this account I was becoming more careless, for one day one of my men, whom I had only just sent out, almost ran right into a force of over a hundred Germans coming straight for our little camp and in a direction from which we had never expected them previously. The man was one of my best askaris and fired two shots to warn us as he made off, but was slightly wounded before he was able to get away in the bush. I was ill in bed at the time and, as I thought before, quite unable to move, but now with one bound I was away down the bamboo-covered slope of a hill after my men, while shots were fired to hurry us on. But the Germans were again deprived of their prey, or the main part of it, for they only got one man who happened to have hurt his leg on one of our night patrols and could not get away quickly enough. The enemy hung around and that afternoon fighting started at long range between them and a Baluchi patrol, which was sometimes sent out as far as my outpost—just to see if we were still alive, I suppose. I cautiously made my way towards the Baluchis to render them assistance, but, as we approached, they thought it was another German force trying to outflank them and we were very nearly fired upon. However, eventually we joined forces and I told the Baluchi N.C.O. in charge, who was not lacking in courage, that I knew of a way by which I could take him to a place overlooking the Germans ; but when we arrived there we found the enemy were retiring, so were only able to get in a few hurried shots at the rearguard.

The Baluchis were out for a fight and wanted to advance still further, till I explained that I thought it was not wise as the nature of the country was unsuitable—and besides, we were only twenty against a hundred. So they returned to their camp at Headquarters and with them they took some of the Germans' exploded cartridges, to show their companions and their officer that they had fought the Germans and made them run.

I with my six men remained on as before, and as the excitement of the fight passed off I had a relapse and felt worse than ever. Fortunately I had sent in my report with the Baluchis and G.H.Q. at last seemed to realize the importance of a strong outpost at Nyandete and I received word that a force of some fifty West African troops with a machine-gun and some native troops, together with my O.C., were coming to relieve me.

A few hours later a stretcher arrived which was to carry me off to hospital. I was borne away by two sturdy blacks from the Ambulance Corps and the next morning, when the sun shone through the stained glass windows, I found myself lying by the altar of a church, which was being used as a clearing hospital, and it was so full of prostrate forms stretched out on the bare ground that there was hardly room for the doctors and attendants to pass between the sufferers.

CHAPTER XXVI

SAILORS ASHORE

THREE days afterwards I heard that the post at Nyandete had been abandoned, that flank now being protected by two companies at a position about half a mile out from the Mission. The following morning, with many others of the worse cases, I was sent back to a hospital nearer the base. This was also full and the tents we were placed in were crowded and terribly hot, so I was glad when a day or so later I was sent back to the base hospital at Kilwa. Here we were housed under a cool building and it was a relief to be able to rest during the day out of the intense heat. I made friends with two sailors, whom I had first seen lying alongside me at the Mission, the one an A.B. and the other a young armourer, and I was glad to see we again occupied the same ward. They were in beds next to mine and used often to pass away the time by relating their experiences.

It appeared that their ship was lying at Kilwa Kisiwani and a Midshipman with two Lewis guns and their crews had been allowed to go inland to assist in the struggle. My two friends spoke of the day when they had heard that they would be amongst the privileged few to go on the great adventure, how they had marched away from the sea with the army one lovely sunny afternoon. But afterwards came disillusion—they had starved ; they had forced-marched until they were footsore ; they had come up against the enemy in skirmishes ; they had night-marched and they had day-marched and then had a bloody battle at Kibata ; they had seen their pals die of pestilence ; at one time they had been on the point of dying of thirst ; they had been out on lonely outposts when the hyenas stole their boots as they slept ; they had heard lions roaming at night and one of them had seen one by day ; they had got fever, they had got everything, including jiggers !

They were overflowing with tales of strange adventures which would hold their shipmates spellbound, though here nobody marvelled at their doings, which were merely everyday events. They now only thirsted for news of their ship, that clean man-o'-war, with its speckless deck and above all the refrigerator ! They often told me of that wonderful refrigerator, where beautiful English vegetables and other luxuries could be kept pure and fresh, even in these reeking tropics. They had never realized the value of the ship's refrigerator until they had to do without green vegetables and were forced to eat meat tainted from the evil air of these low lying parts, to drink water green and crawling with tadpoles and other living things.

All this I gathered from my two bluejacket companions, one a mere boy of eighteen, who from his conversation pined for his ship as only an exile can pine for home. As days went by he grew thinner and thinner and his dysentery worse instead of better and, one night, when all were supposed to be asleep, I noticed the doctor and nurse standing by the bed of their critical patient, for he was not expected to last until the morning. Then they drew away a little and I heard a whispered conference :—

" It is no use, he will never get well here," said the nurse. " The boy is just pining for his ship."

The doctor considered for a moment, then nodded his head and passed on. The nurse tiptoed up to the still bed and said :—

" Be awake early in the morning, Jack, for you are going back to your ship to-morrow. The doctor has just said so."

The next morning as I awoke my eyes turned towards the bed of our little sailor friend. He was now sitting up, his ditty box on his wasted knees as he took from it and anxiously looked at one photo after another. They were mostly of girls he had left behind, far away in many different ports, but he hardly glanced at even the prettiest of them. At last he came to the one he wanted, a battle cruiser, and after gazing at it long he held up the photo for all of us to see.

" This is her, the ' —— ', I am going back to her this morning." And a little later the purring of an ambulance was heard outside and the sister came in hurriedly saying :—

" Are you ready, Jack ? "

" Yes, yes, Sister ! "

The photos disappeared, the ditty box was slammed to and the boy turned and waved us good-bye as he was carried out of the door smiling.

" Some fellows have all the bloomin' luck," said

a gruff voice at my side. "And here am I left behind and with something in my back which is kicking and champing like a cart horse. I never had a wink of sleep all night, or the night before neither, and the doctors say it is only a boil, but I am sure there is something like a devil in there. I can just feel it kicking and going on no end."

With my experience of Africa I diagnosed the armourer's complaint, where even the doctor and nurses had failed.

"Yes, you have something in there all right. There is a certain fly with a bright coloured body, like the bluebottle only with slimmer body and longer legs, which lives near the swamps and if it gets a chance will pierce the skin and lay an egg in you when you are asleep, and that is what has happened to you. The only thing to relieve the irritation is to get the nurse to open the swelling and haul out the lodger."

So the next time the sister came her rounds the armourer told her what I had said and sure enough when she lanced the place out popped a wriggling white maggot, about half an inch long and nearly as thick as a lead pencil.

Relieved of the irritation the sailor dropped off to sleep and I heard him mumbling :—

"You call this a country to live in, where man-eating maggots get under your skin ? Well, I hope they won't say I am a liar when I tell them everything, that's all I hope, I do."

CHAPTER XXVII

PROMOTION TO LIEUTENANT

I REMAINED at Kilwa hospital another week and was then discharged and returned to duty at the front, having been away for almost a month, but was not sent back to Limbanguku. One of the first things I learned when I got back was that I was now promoted to the rank of Lieutenant. My duties were much the same as before, having a commission made very little difference to the work, except perhaps that I carried more weight when attached to a regiment and was able to join in the officers' mess.

Being granted promotion on the field I found the question of kit difficult, although all I really needed was a couple of stars for each shoulder and a Sam Brown belt. But I found it quite impossible to get my stars, until at last I met an old E.A.M.R. friend, now holding a commission in the King's African Rifles, who gave me two spare stars he happened to have, so for a week I walked about with two stars on one shoulder and nothing on the other, until I was encountered by a peppery old Colonel, who demanded to know why I was going about in this lopsided fashion. I explained that I had been promoted in the field and the Ordnance Department did not provide for the needs of newly-made

officers. He readily understood my position and
taking me to his banda presented me with two
more stars which I fixed on to the other shoulder.
The fact that the new ones did not match the first
two was a mere detail—I felt properly dressed at
last.

There was not much doing at the front now,
except minor skirmishes, for the rains had set in
and operations were suspended until the dry
season.

One day a native headman who lived on the
tributary of the Mhambia River asked if I would
shoot a man-eating leopard which was doing considerable damage in his district. As I had little
to do I got a week's leave and accompanied the old
man back to his village. On the way he told me
about the marauder, a large female leopard with
a half-grown cub, and he said it must have learned
the taste of human flesh by eating the wounded
and dead after battle. Now it had come to his
neighbourhood and had already killed three people,
two women and a boy—for whom it had laid in wait
on the outskirts of the village. The last victim was
a woman who was on her way to draw water. The
body had not been removed and the headman told
me that if I watched by it he knew the leopard and
her cub would return that afternoon. He went
on to explain that one of the wounded soldiers the
leopard had eaten must have been a wizard or
medicine man, who now had command of the
animal's body, and if spears were thrown at it the
points bent over as if striking a stone, but he was
sure the white man's bullets would break the spell.

Q

I arrived at the village in the afternoon and was conducted to a prepared platform on a tree near the corpse, for the leopard was in the habit of returning to her kill before sundown. The headman had sent a runner on ahead to have everything ready, so all I had to do was to climb the tree by a rude ladder overlooking the most gruesome corpse of a partly devoured woman, whose staring eyes, set in a head almost severed, seemed to gaze straight towards us as if appealing for revenge. The old man assured me the animal would come soon, for he noticed it had not yet fed on the corpse that day, but I sat for two hours behind a screen of branches and saw nothing. The sun was just hovering on the western horizon when I heard a piercing scream on the other side of the village, and looking in that direction I saw the spotted fiend had pounced on a youth who had run out of the hut to head off two goats, which had broken out of their stall and were making for their pasture. At first I thought of running forward, but realizing that once I left the tree I would lose sight of the leopard until I came right upon the village clearing, and knowing the rapidity with which a man-eating leopard will kill his victim, I decided I must take the risk of killing the boy, and so fired almost automatically. I was glad to see the brute sink down lifeless.

As the echoes of the rifle shot died away there was dead silence perhaps for half a minute. Then doors stealthily opened a few inches as eager black faces peered out from every hut, intently watching to see if the animal would move. The old man brandishing a spear rushed forward—still the leopard did not stir, for it was stone dead, pinning the lad down with its weight. In no time the whole village with yells of delight surrounded the animal, which was pulled off its prey. The lad stood up, opened and shut his eyes and mouth several times and then, rolling his eyes to one side, put his hand up to his neck from which there issued a trickle of blood and at once started to yell " blue murder." I washed the wound with permanganate and found it merely a deep scratch. There were several similar wounds on his woolly head, but luckily for the lad the leopard had been killed almost instantaneously with a head shot, otherwise it might have done considerable damage in its death struggle.

The whole village, especially the older men and women, demonstrated their gratitude in native fashion, and I had a most embarrassing half-hour. Then, as I had a vest-pocket kodak, I cleared the people on one side and took snaps of the leopard and its prospective victim, who had now somewhat recovered from his fright. The old headman, on seeing that I was taking a picture, insisted that I had a photo of myself taken standing by the leopard so that he could have a print to show all comers the English Bwana who had killed the maneater.

I explained that it was impossible for me to take a photo of myself as I had to manipulate the camera, when my own orderly who, as before mentioned, was a German soldier at the beginning of the war, to my great surprise said he understood a camera, for

in peace time he had been the personal servant to
a German planter who had trained him to take
snaps. Every Sunday he was given a rifle and told
to shoot buck, and when he had done so the German,
a very corpulent young man who disliked going
after game himself, would have his photo taken
rifle in hand and foot on the carcass. When the
native shot several buck the German would have
them brought together and strewn carelessly about,
and then have a little tent pitched and a fire lighted
and drink coffee while his photo was taken in
different attitudes. Hamis then showed me how
I must stand, one foot on the victim, chin in air
and an especial faraway look in the eyes, all of
which he demonstrated with great pains.

I was becoming irritated and impatient with him,
and wanted to get the thing over, so showed him
how the camera worked and squatted down behind
the leopard, rifle in hand, and was duly snapped.
The injured youth hovered in the background of
the picture—nothing would induce him to come
nearer to the leopard.

I had never really properly recovered my health
since I left Nyandete, and was now forced to give
in again. I was sent to the local hospital, but grew
worse instead of better. I could not seem to shake
off the malaria at all. One day I was told that I
and about a dozen other officers could go down to
Durban on a special cruise, so that we might be
fit for the big push, which would take place
immediately the rainy season was over. But the
day I was to leave the front I became so ill that I
had to be carried by stretcher to the coast, wheel

transport being entirely out of the question owing to the condition of the roads. We were sent to a place called Mohoro, where a river steamer came up one of the arms of the Rufiji delta. We remained there a few days, and then the boat took us to Dar-es-Salaam, where we boarded a hospital ship and proceeded to Durban.

The sea air and change had done me a lot of good, and when I got to Durban I thought I had recovered, so proceeded to sea-bathe, but the cold water brought out ague again at once and I had to go back to bed. I stayed three weeks in Durban and one week in Johannesburg—a month of utter misery—for more than half the time I spent in bed and the rest in trying to get warm. So when our boat was due to sail I was glad to be going back to the hotter parts. I was ill almost the entire journey, and only stopped getting those horrid cold shivers followed by temperatures when we got back to the tropics.

CHAPTER XXVIII

MEETING OF OLD-TIMERS

AFTER landing from the hospital ship I was allowed to return to duty. I reported to Headquarters and explaining to them I would soon be fit now that I was in a warmer part was told to proceed to Kilwa on a boat sailing in a few days' time. The boat did not get away for a week, however; but Dar-es-Salaam was a pleasant place to kill time in and I still had a lot of strength to build up. Most of the time I had been away in the colder parts I was so malaria-riddled that I could eat little of the sumptuous fare on board ship and in South Africa, owing to constant ague, brought on by the cold.

At our quarters across the bay I met several other agents and officers of the Intelligence Corps ready to go back for the Big Push. One of them from my old corps told me there were several old-timers in town and he said he had brought back from his leave a whole case of the best Cape Brandy, several bottles of which remained. That night he invited two or three friends across the bay to see us, and we were all seated in the long barn-like quarters, previously used by the Germans as an ammunition factory.

" Now, how extraordinary ! We are all old

E.A.M.R.-ites. An occasion like this must be celebrated ! Bar Steward, a large bottle of Champagne, and quick about it ! " And lo and behold, and to the surprise of the visitors, the speaker produced half a dozen bottles of the best South African brandy.

A cork popped, then another and yet another, while our strength was increased by two more of the old corps coming in and the good drink loosened the tongue. We again patrolled the arid country between Oldoinyo Narok and Longido. Again we crossed over the border into a strange and unfamiliar land, then on and on. This talk was strangely mixed with such local news as to who was the last scuppered ? What was Von Lettow doing now ? What was happening on the farm, in far-away British East Africa ? And the best place to get a feed in Dar-es-Salaam ?

Then said the man who was standing the booze and who had just been most annoyed because somebody else asked to be allowed to stand his whack :—

" Look here, I've got an idea. Let us each tell a yarn, but it must be a true one, about the good old days when our shirts were lousy. Who wants to hear all this modern stuff ? " There was a pause and then the speaker continued : " Yes, let each man tell a yarn of the early days, when, as I said, our shirts were suspicious. The good old early days, before our whisky tot was stopped ! After that everything went wrong. They began to civilize us, so to speak, they put us into uniforms, made us cut our hair and beards, took away and burnt our comfy felt hats and put hard helmets on our heads. They took away our trusty little mules and gave us Indian countrybreds, and above all, they made us drill and salute our officers, and even wash our shirts ! Now, who is going to tell a story of the good old early days ? Stand up on your hind legs, someone, and let us have it ! "

A long, lanky coffee farmer, now an N.C.O. in the Livestock, whose bare arms were bronzed by exposure to sun, stood up unsteadily amidst much applause and, making a motion for silence, cleared his throat.

." Ladies and Gentlemen—ah, excuse me, I didn't exactly mean either. . . ."

" Stiffs and Scallywags of the E.A.M.R. ! " shouted a man who had hitherto kept silence.

" Well then, Sciffs and Stallywags of the E.A.M.R., what I want to say is that it is not a story I have to tell——"

" Boo, Boo ! "

" But wait a moment, don't be so impatient ! I will tell one presently, but I propose that J—— over there, who is standing all the strong drink, first of all tells us how our whisky ration got stopped."

" Hear, hear ! " Great applause and stamping of feet.

" Well, stand up then, J——."

" Well, one day in 1915, the Governor of British East Africa, hearing of the wickedness of the settler soldiers at Bissel camp on the border, decided to send a Padre out to guide them back into the paths of righteousness and our hero was appointed

to the rank of military chaplain for the purpose.
He hurried off to a Goan tailor, who measured
him in every direction and a week later he stood
up in every detail a fighting officer, except for his
dog-collar. Then for the hazardous journey out
to Lone Hill and Longido ! Nobody saw him
come and it is to this day not known if he came on
mule-back or ox wagon. Some said mule, but
others declared it was ox, for if he came by mule
he surely would have been seen at the dressing-
station having his half-crowns dressed, as was the
custom of all new-comers after the jogging ride.
But no matter how he came, he was there, though
nobody took much notice of him, for we had our
own Padre, the Rev. Cobham, who preached to
us on a Sunday in a way we best understood, did
duties of a corporal during the week-days and was
always able to take his place in the ring when there
was a boxing tournament on. Neither was he too
uppish to join in a camp sing-song. You fellows
will all remember Cobham, quite a youngster and
the whitest man in the war. He was killed in
action, when carrying a wounded askari out under
heavy fire. The new and official padre hovered
about camp for a day or so, speaking of our sins and
preaching a sermon, which practically nobody
turned up to. On the whole he could not have
been very highly impressed with the settlers who
were defending the border, for he hardly stayed
a week before he proceeded to return to Nairobi
and reported to high authority terrible stories of
our drunkenness, as a result of the peg of whisky at
sundown. . . . ' I never heard of such a thing,

preposterous ! Who ever heard of British soldiers being issued with spirits ? There are the flower of East Africa's young men being deliberately educated to strong drink, etc. etc.' The matter was taken up seriously, however, and no more cases of Johnny Walker went out to the border, at least by way of soldier's rations. Don't I remember the day well ? " said the speaker thoughtfully. " I had just been on a long day's patrol towards Kilimanjaro, had rubbed down my mule, tied him on the lines with a feed at the end of his nose and then, having had a wash, I glanced towards the west and my tired heart leapt lightly with joy, for that golden orb was just dancing on the horizon and soon would dip below the thorn-tree-fringed kopje. Then the Quartermaster would shout, ' Roll up, roll up, lads, for your tots,' and proceed to issue our nightly peg, which up to the present we had had regularly every night, except once when the Quartermaster got drunk. So I took from my haversack my mug and, rubbing off the dust of the day's patrol, I strolled towards the rickety grass-shed which did us as Q.M. Stores at Bissel. Before I got there I knew something had gone wrong, for there was old ex-colonel McClure, now serving as a Lance-Corporal, and old Charlieboy, a regular with twenty-one years' service behind him in the British Army and as many years as a freebooter in China, perhaps even another twenty of unknown occupation, with Tim Lane and others, sitting on biscuit cases with faces as long as Kongonis. ' Whatever has happened ! ' said I. ' Have the Germans gained a great victory in Europe ? ' ' No !

Worse ! ' said Lance-Corporal McClure, as he licked his parched lips. ' What, worse ? The Germans have not landed in England, surely ? ' ' No, but I wish to Heaven they had landed in Nairobi and chased around a certain Sky Pilot we know ! ' "

" To sad, too sad ! " called out a raucous voice. " We want something cheerful. Have another drink, anyway, to cheer you up."

There was a slight pause, then the man on my right said :

" Mentioning Tim Lane reminds me of the story about him at Bissel."

" Out with it, then ! " came a chorus.

" But it is sad, too."

" Out with it, anyway."

" Well, as you know, Tim Lane was a B. Squadron man, a little middle-aged fellow with a piping voice. In private life he was one of those ne'er-do-wells and now at a ripe middle-age he had wandered over the face of Africa. He was always talking about having been in Abyssinia and the ' Sowerdown Improvidence ' as he expressed it, meaning the Sudan Province ; but how he got there and came away again is a mystery. However, he often got the young recruits around him and told them stories of his doings in Abyssinia and other wild places, which set them open mouthed in wonderment. You'd hear him begin with impressive gestures, ' Well, when I was away down in the Sowerdown Improvidence I came to a fertile land ruled by a very rich and mighty Arab queen, but she was impregnable. . . .' So the story went. Some time after Tim's arrival, however (the Queen,

who was quite white and very beautiful, according
to his description), was blessed with a son and
heir, and our friend Lane became the first man in
all the country and sat at the right hand of the
Queen's throne on Court days. Then would follow
a long description as to the life at an imaginary
court somewhere up towards Abyssinia. One day
Tim Lane was telling a story of game shooting—
how many buffaloes and elephants he had not shot
in his beloved Sowerdown Improvidence, when an
old Uganda hunter, Gould by name, said he
believed he had not seen, much less shot, a buffalo
in his life, and then related to Tim's audience
the story of how he and Tim Lane, while on
advance guard to a patrol that very morning, had
seen right in their path a small herd of wildebeest.
The animals were tossing their heads and waving
their tails as only wildebeest do. Tim Lane spotted
them and said : ' Buffalo, they will attack us ! '
and refused to go on another yard. When we got
back the old hunter chaffed poor Tim to death
in front of his own audience, which only a few
moments ago had been listening to the marvels
of his doings with awe and wonderment, so that
now even the Arab queen lost her attraction.

" The story about him and the wildebeest got
around, and on several occasions during the day
fun was poked from unexpected quarters. Although
with his Cockney wit he gave back as good as he
received, he soon became depressed and melancholy.
Towards the evening he again met Gould, who
immediately said: ' And now what would your
Arab queen have thought of you had she seen

you and the wildebeest this morning?' Tim
stepped forward and in a dramatic voice, as if
addressing a large audience, said : ' I suppose you
all think I am a coward ? But I do not fear death.
Now I will show you that I am not afraid to face
bullets.' Tim paused here to let what he had
said sink in and then continued : ' At ten o'clock
to-night you will say little Tim has kept his
word ! ' He then turned round dramatically as if
ending an act and with an air of importance
strolled away while everyone else went about their
business, thinking nothing more of the matter.
But precisely at ten o'clock, when most of the men
had dropped off to sleep and the rest were dozing,
suddenly in the stillness of the night a shot echoed
from one of the tents.

" I grasped my rifle and throwing on an overcoat
went outside, expecting an attack by the enemy.
A little knot of men had gathered at the door of
one of the tents of B. Squadron lines. A few
strides brought me there, and looking inside, I
saw Tim Lane lying on his back on a ground-sheet
in the middle of the tent. He seemed quite calm,
but was lying in a pool of blood with a Service
revolver close beside him. Then he spoke as if
to himself and partly addressing an audience :
' Done it again ! There's me gone and made a
bloomin' mistake again and I was sure my heart
was on my right side here when I shot and now it
must have been on the left, for I am not dead, nor
feel like dying, but I suppose I shall be a gorner
soon ! '

" Captain Douglas, the B. Squadron commander,

then came up and we made room for him to enter.
' Turn the poor fellow over, Sergeant, and let us
see where he is hit,' were his precise words. ' No
need for that,' said Trooper Tim in his usual
dramatic way, and with these words he sat up with
a jerk, for all the world as if he were again play-
acting. ' This is where the bullet went in, and this
is where it bloomin' well came out,' indicating a
blood-sodden patch on his back. ' Now, do you
think Little Tim is a coward, ha ? In a little while
Tim will be dead. Then just throw him outside
the camp to the jackals—there is no need for a
burial—Little Tim, he will be all right with the
jackals ! '

" A doctor was hurriedly summoned and while
he was coming Captain Douglas thought it was his
duty to make enquiries about the dying man's
next of kin. ' You have a daughter, have you not,
Trooper Lane ? Is there any message you would
like us to give her ? ' Tim lay and looked hard
at our Captain's face, then said with a twinkle of
the eye and a grin : ' No, my daughter is a son,
and a better man than you will ever be. . . .
There is no message. Just throw me out to the
little jackals when I have snuffed my last, I know
they are hungry.' "

Here the narrator paused and there was a few
moments' silence, when a newcomer said :—

" And what happened to him eventually ? Did
they throw him out to the jackals ? "

" No blooming fear ! Tim was not the sort
to die. Dr. Wilson came along, plugged up his
holes with cotton-wool and iodine. The 4.50

bullet, large as it was, had not touched any really vital spot. Tim only wanted to shock the youngsters."

" Next, please," said the man who was standing the drinks. " Who is going to tell the next yarn ? Come on, then, someone. Here, have a drink to loosen your tongue."

" Here, steady, give the fellows a chance to think. Can't you see by all their puckered brows that everyone of them is just bursting with stories, but does not know which is the best one to tell ? Come on, now, out with something someone ! "

All the puckered brows lit up simultaneously and three narrators started off at once.

" Here, one at a time, please ! You are the soberest and oldest, so go ahead and let the two youngsters come next."

The narrator with a slightly grizzled beard, but the twinkle of youth in his eyes, started :—

" Well, right at the beginning of the war the old corps was a queer mixture, you know. Some dressed this way and others that. Some never washed and changed their clothes, and others were always washing, even if they had not a change of clothes. Well, the fellow I am going to tell you about, Long H——, you will remember, was one of the clean ones. In fact, I think he would without any contradiction be called the cleanest man in the E.A.M.R. At the beginning nobody was blamed for not washing, for water was by no means plentiful and sometimes there was hardly enough to drink, but H—— always managed to get a wash somehow. Some said that on a long thirsty patrol it was a toss-up as to whether he used his water for outside ablutions or internal lubrication.

" When we were camped at the Kidongai River, H—— went down to the clear stream to bathe every day, never less than four times and sometimes six and each time would invariably inspect his undervest, wash it, and, as it was the only one he had, stand about until it dried in the sun, and the boys swore he would only get back to camp in time to go down for another bathe ! When we reached the Manga River the first thing I remember seeing was H——'s six foot odd standing stripped, ankle deep in the stream.

" A week later we were ordered on a very long patrol, which would take us over the waterless plain to the north of Kilimanjaro, which as you know is in most places a waste of volcanic ash, except where the lava covers the plains for miles in the form of loose rocks. We rode on day and night until we at last came to some muddy, slimy water and in no time H—— had his shirt off and was standing ankle-deep on the edge of the foul water, but his nerve must have failed him this time, for he returned to the other men and sat down disconsolately under the doubtful shade of some thorn trees. At the next pool we came to H—— was also foiled, for when all the men and mules had drunk their fill, there was nothing left but a few homeless frogs and unhappy crabs.

" For several days past I must here confess I had felt somehow that all was not well under my shirt, but modesty kept me from saying a word, and I was only able to scratch occasionally when oppor-

. . . LARGE STORES OF GRAIN WERE FOUND

[p. 278.

AFRICA'S RAW MATERIAL IN MILITARY TRAINING

[p. 285.

tunity occurred, as I felt I was the only one who was thus afflicted and was ashamed not to have washed more frequently. My mind, however, was a little relieved when one day I surprised our Sergeant-Major, also a scrupulously clean man, behind some bushes with his shirt off, suspiciously picking numerous objects from his undervest.

" At last we came to a clear stream of bubbling water and hastened to make camp near it. You may be sure not only Long H——, but many others hastily threw aside their clothes and bathed in the refreshing water. When nobody was looking, I hastily removed my undervest, rolled it up so that none might see what it contained, and quickly shoved it under water, in hopes of drowning the little beggars. Thus I stood with one foot on the garment when I saw H—— inspecting his vest, and I noticed a look of horror slowly steal over his face as he dropped the garment to the ground. Then screwing up courage he picked it up and strode off to our Lieutenant, who was an old Boer War campaigner.

" ' Sir, what are these on my undervest ? ' said H—— in his direct way. ' Lice, my boy,' said the officer, in a matter-of-fact voice and then with a knowing twinkle in the eye, he added: ' Fancy you being the first man to get them ! Lousy H—— ! ' When the news got around that lice had been found on H——'s vest, nobody was ashamed to admit having found them."

Hardly had the narrator finished his yarn when there was another man ready with the next.

" Reminds me of some queer tent-mates of mine

R

in the early days. When war broke out I rushed off to Nairobi to join up like everybody else. I was hurriedly sworn in as if there was not a moment to spare and then sent to camp on the race-course for weeks. I remember that day well. I was told by the Sergeant-Major to go into a certain tent in which he said there were only three fellows, which was lucky for me, as some of the other tents had four or five in them already.

" When I arrived there I saw two of my future tent-mates seated on the floor ; a little middle-aged man with a red face and nose, wearing a large aquascutum coat of peculiar design and innumerable pockets, and next to him a younger man, sturdily built with dark hair and a Jewish countenance, wearing khaki flannel shirt, shorts and golf stockings. As I approached the tent door the two pairs of eyes followed my every movement, but not a word was spoken. ' I hope you fellows don't mind my coming in here ? ' said I, cheerily. ' The Sergeant-Major says it is the only vacancy, you know.' Immediately the jaws of the man in the golf stockings began to work and then words came out : ' You are w-w-welcome, but I am afraid y-y-y-you will have to sleep in the t-t-tent fly. F-f-fullup-inside ! ' So I deposited my kit under the fly and sat down.

" The two men only took an occasional glance at me as they busied themselves with opening a tin of Huntley and Palmer's biscuits, ready for their tea. When the air-tight lid was removed, the little man in the aquascutum coat rushed out, calling out ' Njorogi, Njorogi,' scanned the horizon, shook his

head and then disappeared round the corner and
soon returned with a boiling billycan dangling from
a stick. This he placed in the middle of the tent
swiftly, yet so dexterously that none of the liquid
was spilt. He drew open the flap of his coat and
I noticed that it contained many little pockets
inside as well. From one of these he took out a
small quantity of tea leaves and dropped them into
the boiling water. Then from another he took out
something else and after stirring for a small space
of time, he drew from another pocket a phial of
white powder, the merest pinch of which he
deposited into the billycan, with the air of one who
knows what he is about, and continued to stir.

" He then seemed to notice me for the first time
and looking in my direction, his jaws and then the
muscles of his neck appeared to be working as if
under great strain. ' Lord ! ' thought I to myself,
' Surely this one does not stutter, too ? ' But he
did, indeed, and worse than the first one. At last
after terrible efforts the words came : ' H-h-have a
drink of tea. H-h-have some tea, will you ? ' ' Thank
you,' said I, ' it is indeed kind of you.' ' N-n-not-
atall, you are welcome.' But in spite of the
hospitality, I somehow felt I was an intruder and
not wanted. ' Not quite s-s-sweet enough,' said
the man in the golf stockings. Whereupon the other
produced from his wonderful coat the miniature
bottle and inserting the blade of a pen-knife, took
from the phial another pinch of saccharine, which
he placed in the friend's tea, quickly corked the
bottle and methodically put it back in its pocket.
It was said that he was a vegetarian and could

live off the contents of that coat for two weeks exactly.

"Looking in my direction, he said: 'Y-y-you know, t-t-two daysago a hy-hy-hee-hee-hee——' 'Hyena,' said the man in the golf stockings, looking at me with meaning in his eyes. The little man's red face grew redder than ever and he turned upon his companion with anger, saying : ' Oh, th-thank you, b-b-but you are no-no-no gentleman ! ' Then turning to me where he was interrupted, said : ' T-t-two nights ago, a hy-hy-hee-hee '—his companion was again about to supply the word, but caught the other's eye in time, so helped himself to another biscuit instead, when the first continued : ' T-T-two nights ago, a hy-hy-he-hena took a p-p-pound of steak f-f-from that fly, you, you mustbecareful ! ' His friend in the golf stockings, who was nothing like such a bad stutterer, explained that hyena prowled about the camp at night and advised me to find other quarters where I could sleep inside a tent. So I continued listening to a few stories—this time of a ravenous lion which lived in the neighbourhood—with such a calm that I could see it annoyed my informants. Then coolly arranging my blankets in the form of a pillow, I lay down to have an afternoon rest.

"Quiet and peace reigned over the camp, the man with the golf stockings retired with his back against a large kitbag, reading a magazine, while the little red-faced man started arranging and rearranging various articles in his numerous pockets, till he drew from his trousers hip-pocket a little bag of shelled monkey-nuts and solemnly began to devour them one by one, inspecting each one as he did so. I was just dozing off, wondering if this was a fair sample of the E.A.M.R., when the right leg of the man in the golf stockings shot out violently, as if to kick somebody. I looked round. The man in the coat continued to eat his nuts, taking not the least notice. Even the other's expression altered not in the least, nor did he take his eyes off the print before him. The whole thing seemed so uncanny that sleep was out of the question and between my partly closed eyes I watched that leg and on two different occasions did it suddenly shoot out as though kicking at an imaginary mosquito. The leg seemed to be working independently of its owner, whose face remained placid, reading his magazine.

" Suddenly I noticed a red-fezzed toto flit by the tent, giving one very sheepish glance inside— then disappearing. The man in the golf stockings came to life with one bound, collared the toto by the scruff of the neck and boxed his ears soundly, all the time stuttering curses in Swahili and every other native language, in between which he fiercely gnashed his teeth. In this way he worked himself into a terrible rage and the toto fared pretty badly. At last he came back panting and said he must go to Nairobi at once. The trouble with R—— was that when he lost his temper he used to gnash his teeth so hard that he generally broke his plate ! This was my first experience of the old corps," said the speaker. " I stayed on in that tent for some weeks and by George, when I went home on leave my mother declared I stammered, too ! "

The hour was now long past midnight, the Cape brandy was finished and the man who had been standing it had subsided beneath the table where he slumbered peacefully enough on the floor. The small crowd had by this time increased by a few more, but one or two took no further interest in their surroundings, having become more or less incapacitated. We were all about to break up and retire, when lo and behold, an I.D. Agent produced half a dozen bottles of real champagne as if from nowhere.

" Come on, you chaps, we will drink four of these bottles, but keep two as a prize, to be sent to the man who in our opinion deserves the most merit for looting. Not the man who tells the loot story, oh no ! That would not be quite fair, for I know some of you fellows could stretch a yarn pretty far for a bottle or two of phiz. Now, come on, the next man for a loot story. You know there have been some pretty tough nuts fighting out here in this war, so you should not have any difficulty."

Again several men started off simultaneously, but eventually all but one were quietened down.

" Yes, let me see, loot—I think the best fellow I know for loot is Lieutenant X——, in the I.D. It was about February this year when he went about things scientifically. First of all he looted a wagon from a German farm, then he looted some slaughter oxen from our own commissariat. These were on the way to the front, and as they happened to be old work oxen he yoked them up. By this time he had also collected a pretty good supply of miscellaneous articles in various ways, not only from different German farmhouses, but wherever he could pick them up. These he camouflaged into cases of ammunition and equipment, marked for the I.D. front line. He had more sense, mark you, than to disguise his booty as rations ! Then he put his best native N.C.O. in charge, a real blood drinker of a fellow. So no one interfered much with that wagon, and as days went on it became more and more bulky."

" What did it contain ? " said the man guarding the two bottles of champagne, who had now taken up the attitude of an umpire, and a very officious one too.

" Well, let me see now, I could not give you an absolute detailed list."

" You must give some sort of a list, for this will bear greatly on the prize for merit. Now come on, quick, a rough list."

" Of course, I did not inspect each article in detail, but from what I gathered there was a pair of fine ivory tusks, disguised as a bundle of tenting and taken from a German homestead ; two leopard skins nicely mounted on green baize ; many silver dishes—including, I remember, a large soup tureen, all charred black to look like base metal ; a feather bed ; a double bedstead in native carved teak— dismantled of course ; two brand-new saddles taken from some South African mounted infantrymen whom he found resting by the roadside ; two cases of British army boots, which had mysteriously disappeared just before they were about to be issued; one case of local German whisky—very raw and strong stuff, I believe—they used to give it to their askaris before a charge and called it ' Fixed Bayonets ' brand."

" You seem to be well informed. How did you know all this ? " said the umpire scrutinizing the relater very closely. " I should not be surprised if you had a finger in the pie."

" And I might tell you that you're taking up the attitude of a blooming judge, trying to convict a fellow. Remember I'm merely telling the story. As a matter of fact I saw the list afterwards, when X—— got into trouble——"

" Ah—hh. Then your man did not get away with his loot. Got into trouble, did he ? I'm afraid that will have a distinct bearing on my final summing up. How many years did he get ? "

" I think it was two."

" Next man, please."

" Just a moment, it was not for this offence that X—— was hauled up."

" Well, what was it for, then ? "

" If you'd only let me get on with the story and not talk so much yourself, I might tell you. Where was I ? Oh, yes, well Lieutenant X—— finding his oxen dying of tsetse fly away up in the heart of conquered territory and his wagon likely to be stranded there any moment, applied for a transfer to the Political Department and was made Political Officer in charge of the very district he was then in. So he stepped straight into his new job, complete with wagon. The British army rolled on driving the Huns before it and Lieutenant X—— was left peacefully behind to administrate the natives. He stowed his wagon load of goods snugly

in his capacious Administrative Headquarters.
Now that little move, getting into the Political I
think, will take some beating for merit," said the
narrator, looking for approval at the man with
the two bottles.

" Go ahead with your story, is there more ? "

"Oh, all right—where did I get to ? Ah, yes, X——
is an Administrative Officer in charge of a fertile
district teeming with industrious agricultural natives.
Nearby his post was a cluster of ramshackle Indian
dukas, who had resided many years in the district
and become exceedingly rich, especially one man
called Ramji, or Rami, or something like that—I
am not quite sure but I know it had a ram in it.
Well, Ramji had two wives whom before the war
he used as his bank, that is to say, if he had any
spare coins he would melt them down into jewelry,
which he could fasten securely to the ankles, arms
or ears of the women. Ramji held forth to his
cronies that this was the only way of saving money,
for a woman naturally had to be watched as carefully as any spare coins, so why not kill two birds
with one stone ? Also the great advantage of this
method, he said, was that the richer you got the
more you put round her ankles and the less chance
she had of running off with another man. Well,
just before the war it appears that Ramji's wives
had become so heavily laden that he was seriously
thinking of getting a third, in fact had already
entered into negotiations when war was declared,
and panic stricken he buried all his wealth in a
secret hiding-place. Now Administrative Officer
X—— had not been in the place a week when he

knew all about Ramji and his domestic affairs. Of course, being an ex-Intelligence officer no doubt helped him a lot and it was through coveting this very jewelry and the methods he used in trying to extort the secret of their whereabouts from Ramji that he got himself into trouble. When he found he could get nothing out of the old Indian he ordered that the floor of Ramji's shop and dwelling house should be dug up. Now poor Ramji was greatly upset and, as he afterwards said, he was not a mere *shenzi* to be treated in this way, so he and his friends drafted out a long letter and sent it to the British Administrative Headquarters."

Several more stories of loot were told, some dull and others entertaining. Only two of them, said the umpire, appeared really to have any merit. The one was of a young Scotch N.C.O. who had looted from a German plantation a five-section iron harrow, weighing a third of a ton, as well as a water wheel weighing about two tons, and it was decided all round that he was some considerable fellow. The other was an officer who looted a full sized piano, a four-wheeled pony carriage, six Arusha geese, a dachshund and a meat safe, as well as a few cooking utensils.

There was a good deal of discussion as to which of the three deserved the prize. Some decided in favour of X——, others said they were sure a man who could get away with a two-ton water wheel deserved some consideration. So a committee of three was appointed and the man with the two bottles was now officially declared umpire. He first ruled out Lieutenant X—— as he had been so clumsy as to get caught by the long arm of the law.

" Now," said the umpire, " the merit lies between the young Scotsman and the officer who looted the piano and geese, etc. Now what has our informant of the water-wheel story to say ? How are we to be sure that the young Scot got the two-ton water wheel from conquered territory to B.E.A. ? "

It was here asserted that more than one present had seen the water wheel, a large, massive affair, at Moshi and again at a later period had seen it working on the young Scotsman's farm in Kenya. In fact he had been able to take on a Government posho contract.

" This," said one of the committee, " should be one up for the Scotsman."

For it had not only been asserted that the two-ton water wheel and fittings had been transported secretly in some mysterious way from Moshi to Kenya, but transported intact. Had it not just been said that the machine was seen grinding posho for a Government contract, which means that it was grinding well and which proves that the piece of machinery, though, massive was transported with such care as not to damage or deteriorate its grinding qualities as a posho mill.

The umpire making a note of these details, proceeded :—

" Now for the—let me see, how many sections did the harrow have ? "

" Five," came the prompt reply.

" Now, it is also said that the Scotsman looted a five-section harrow, weighing what was it ? "

" About a third of a ton."

" Before going any further," said the umpire.
" I should like the gentleman over there to explain
why the harrow had five sections and not three."

He went on to explain that he was a planter
himself, having harrowed many an acre of land,
and all the harrows he had seen were made up in
three sections.   It was little flaws like this, insigni-
ficant as they appear, which sometimes exposed the
biggest frauds ever committed.   So, reluctant as
he was, he must press the point.

After this hot words followed between the umpire
and the supporters of the Scotsman's story, and as
one of them appeared likely to give the umpire a
licking then and there it was unanimously agreed
that the Germans made their harrows in five sections.   Peace having been restored, the company
relit cigarettes as the umpire continued :—

" Will the relater of the harrow story please tell
us what proof he has that the young Scotsman
successfully looted the five-section harrow ?   As in
the case of the water wheel, did he first see it in
enemy's territory and then later working on the
Scotsman farm in B.E.A. ?   Was the owner also
able to obtain a Government ploughing contract
through its usefulness ? "

Here the man addressed stood up, leaning
heavily on the back of a chair and said :—

" I have every proof that what I say is true," and
immediately sat down again and continued :—

" During the war I was in the Livestock Department—Milligan's crowd, you know. I was stationed
at our Headquarters when several urgent messages

came from a young Scots Sergeant in charge of
some cattle hundreds of miles inland. All the
messages were to the effect that he must have more
porters at once. Would they send him more boys
immediately? Well, our O.C. not being a fool
took no notice of the messages, knowing that the
N.C.O. had plenty of boys. Nothing more was
heard of the *shauri* then for the German General
Tafel had broken back that way and somewhat
scattered the young Scotsman's party ; but later
on when old Tafel was captured, one of his officers
said that he had come upon the young Scotsman's
kit, which had been abandoned by his frightened
porters. The Germans naturally went through it
and great was their surprise when they found in
this place, miles and miles from civilization or any
farming industries, a complete five-section harrow,
which showed signs of having been laboriously
carted by sweating porters. Also, by the way,
another strange thing amongst the man's kit was
the title deeds of a farm in B.E.A. These the German
officers duly handed back to the correct quarters ;
but they said they could not understand how the
English N.C.O.'s were able to carry agricultural
implements and title deeds with them when most
men on their side found great difficulty in carrying
adequate supplies and necessaries of life."

" So the young Scotsman did not get away with
his harrow ? "

" Not according to the German officers' records,
but quite probably when Tafel's lot passed on he
went back for it. It is not likely that he would

abandon it altogether after carrying it all those hundreds of miles."

" Now," said the umpire, " will you over there give me more details about the officer who took the geese and piano ? What proof have you of the correctness of your story ? "

" I was staying with this officer only the other day, both of us on leave you know, and I saw the geese on his lawn and the piano in his drawing-room. What more proof do you want than that ? "

" Well, you have not told us yet how he looted the things."

" When the Germans had been driven back from the neighbourhood of Arusha and the Tanga line, there were a considerable number of vacant houses to be found with such things as pianos in the front rooms and carriages in the outhouses, dachshunds walking about homeless and geese meandering. Now our officer was at this time serving in a fighting unit and was greatly grieved to see all these things going to waste, so he made up his mind to have some of them. By some unrecorded strategy he got himself transferred to the Remount Department. So there he was, left behind to send on remounts and with loot galore around him. Being in authority and right on the railway, he had no difficulty in sending anything he got hold of, such as cottage pianos, disguised as cases of condemned horse rations. But here I must give some information which I am sure will go greatly to the credit of this officer. Immediately he had finished up the loot, or very soon after, he scarified his cushy job and made arrangements to get back to the front line with his old corps. By this time slight changes had come about. All the horses had died of tsetse fly so the old corps was no more, having been absorbed by various foot regiments ; but our officer being of the fighting breed, was determined to get back to the firing line somehow. So he enlisted in a newly formed battalion of the K.A.R. and lived to see many more sharp skirmishes with the enemy."

" I don't see that this has got anything to do with the merit of a looter," said the umpire. " The point is, did he ever get hauled up for looting ? "

" No."

" Ever get into trouble for it ? "

" Certainly not ! "

" Well, that shows more merit than having gone back to the firing line, for it proves that he was practical in his method. I think he almost deserves the prize. But then again, he had a railway at his disposal and condemned horse feed as an excuse for sending back bulky goods, whereas the young Scot had miles of almost desert country over which to laboriously carry his harrow. Of course, in the case of the water wheel he was near a railway, but then he was not an officer in authority and had no condemned horse rations to send back. Nobody knows how he got the booty to his farm. The mere fact that no trace of his methods was discovered, proves his powers of discretion and ingenuity. I am about to——"

" What about the geese and the dachshund ? " said a rosy faced man, raising his voice to drown everyone else. " I am sure a man who can loot such things without a stain on his tunic deserves

a little consideration. Now think of it, there you
are with six Arusha geese and a strange dachshund, who might bite at any moment. You can't
send them as condemned horse feed, for being
noisy creatures they would soon give the game away
and become railway official feed, the geese anyway, for everyone as you know has a weakness
for a fat goose. You could not put them in your
uniform case, perched on your best tunic. Moreover, you will remember the geese in mention were
Arusha geese, a particularly fierce breed. Last time
I visited the house of our friend I was chased round
the lawn before dinner——"

"I rule out this man's evidence," said the
umpire, "for has he not himself admitted he dines
with the officer and no doubt would welcome the
champagne? What more proof do you want than
that? No doubt he would split the drink with his
man. Gentlemen, I award the prize to the young
Scot."

Next morning the opal-tinted dawn shed itself
over the slumbering harbour of Dar-es-Salaam.
Then the sun came out, peeping through the
shutterless windows of the I.D. barracks, and there,
restlessly tossing to and fro, I saw the thorn-scarred,
sunburned limbs of an I.D. officer. Presently the
owner, a young man, rubbed his eyes and slowly
sat up in bed.

"Oh, my God, what a thirst!"

"Yes, what a damnable thirst!" came the echo
from the neighbouring bed.

"And what a throat I have," said J—— of the

previous night, as he slowly came to life. " Yes—
let me see—oh, of course, it was a party."

Then the two pairs of eyes with but one thought
behind them turned simultaneously to the chop
box, where stood side by side two rare golden
capped bottles.

" Of course, we could get fresh ones to send
him."

" Yes, of course," came the ready reply. " After
all, don't you think we did talk a lot of tommyrot
last night ? "

CHAPTER XXIX

THE ADVANCE ON NARENGOMBI

I RETURNED to Kilwa. The great push started on all fronts and we began to move inland again, driving the Germans before us, but not without occasional stubborn resistance. For whenever the enemy found themselves in a good position they fought desperately, and as they were able to choose their ground I think we generally suffered the most casualties.

My duties in this advance were much as before—to find out about the country ahead and get local guides. I was kept so busy that I had no time to think about illness. When the column halted for a day or so I would go out scouting, and often by making a circular movement get into country occupied by the enemy's forces. There I would wait on some path and kidnap any isolated natives going along. Sometimes it would only be a porter or two carrying rations, sometimes a stray askari, but they would all yield some useful information if handled the right way. One of my greatest difficulties when doing advance guards was to keep the guides when the bullets began to fly; for they were not used to our mode of battle and would invariably dive into the nearest bush or long grass and never be seen again. It was a very serious matter for all if we lost our only guide, as the maps of these parts were very rough and so little was known of the country that the army could not march until a new guide was found.

A ludicrous sight it often would have seemed, if the situation were not so grave. One would be walking along a path with some ragged-looking wretch of a local native, the company doing advance guard extended in open formation to right and left, the main body with the Commander half a mile back, which was the typical formation adopted in the East African campaign. We would presently be approaching suspicious-looking country, but dare not waste time in reconnoitring ; for we, the advance guard, were after all merely a buffer of the larger force and the General behind expected us to push on and take blows. Without a second's warning machine-gun and rifle fire would burst out right in front of us and everyone would drop to the ground as one man, some never to rise again, but the majority merely taking cover. The wretched guide would take one glance around for the nearest bush, but the Intelligence officer, expecting this, would hang on to the black man like grim death as they both lay down in the nearest cover, never for a second relaxing his grip until perhaps his orderly would come to his assistance and take over the guide. If the affair was to be a mere ambush by a small body of enemy sent to worry the advancing column, they would soon be driven back ; but if it were to be a big affair the main body would come up and there would follow a pitched battle, perhaps lasting only a few hours, perhaps several

days. But a wise Intelligence officer would never
let his guide get out of sight, for he would be needed
again before the column could move forward.

At one section on this push, when I was doing
the advance guard for the column, we were
ambushed as often as two or three times a day and
I cannot think of anything quite so nerve wracking
as having to do this sort of thing for a week on end,
owing to shortage of Intelligence officers through
illness. The various companies took it in
turns to supply the men for the advance guard
each day, but the unfortunate Intelligence officer,
unless he had someone to relieve him or was
lucky enough to be with K.A.R. troops who
could speak Swahili, had to be in front with his
guide every day. The guides also had a pretty
rough time, but fortunately it was fairly easy to
provide relays. Before this particular trip was over
I had collected about half a dozen local natives,
the spare ones coming along behind with the baggage, when they could be drawn upon if the man
in front got hit, or, more frequently, escaped into
the bush.

The natives in these parts, though in sympathy
with the British I think, did not care very much
which side won and unlike those I had had to deal
with farther north, would not voluntarily offer to
enter into any dangerous undertaking ; but I
think it was only from timidity and not because
they did not want to help us, for I found all their
information most extraordinarily accurate and
generally helpful.

As days went by we neared the German main

prepared position, Narengombi. The country became less hilly but more waterless. Narengombi had been chosen by the enemy because it was ideally situated for a large engagement, and also held the only water-hole for miles around. So the attacking force must either win the day or retire for water.

As the various smaller German forces had joined up to concentrate on this position, so did we— following at their heels and now consisting of one large force, under Colonel Orr, who was acting Brigadier.

On reaching the main column I joined up with other Intelligence officers, including the I.D. Captain in charge of the Intelligence for the whole force. The night before the battle I was sent out with a small party of men and was lucky enough to come across a local native who had actually been working inside the German position and he was able to give me valuable information. I did not venture too near the German lines myself, however, for the native also gave me timely warning about concealed pickets.

The next morning No. 1 and No. 2 columns advanced and were at once heavily engaged ; and the battle raged, neither side giving ground. Later on I received orders to report to the General and was told to guide No. 3 column, about a thousand strong, under a Colonel Taylor, who were to attack the enemy's extreme left flank, drive it back and take Narengombi water-hole. This column which had been lying in reserve was already in prepared formation and when I reported to the Colonel he told me to go forward to the advance guard, which was being done by a K.A.R. company under a Captain Webb. On reaching the place I was surprised to find that Captain Webb was my old E.A.M.R. Squadron Leader, whom I had not seen since the days of the fighting on the Tanga railway.

We moved forward only to come upon a very strong prepared position and we were at a great disadvantage for whereas the Germans were safely behind their raised earthworks, which were so well camouflaged with dry grass as to look exactly like the surroundings, our troops had to lie down on the exposed ground. For hours the battle raged until at last the column had to fall back owing to the large number of casualties. However, the other two columns held their ground and that night the Germans retired, fearing a renewed attack in the morning. It was evident that they had meant to hold out for some time at Narengombi, for large stores of grain were found, which the enemy had set fire to and tried to destroy at the last moment.

Although the battle ended in a victory for us, we paid heavily for it, the casualties being some six hundred, almost a quarter of the entire troops engaged. The Germans took up another position some miles back, but we were too hard hit to attack immediately without reorganization. So the troops rested, encamped at the water-hole.

At Narengombi I also met another distinguished personage of the E.A.M.R., Major Clifford Hill, who towards the end had been Commander of the old corps. Since entering the tsetse fly belt all his horses had died and his ranks were now widely scattered, some as officers of the K.A.R. and other local units, though many succumbed to illness and fighting, but it was good to see our Major still up in the front lines.

The next day Captain Percival, who was now in charge of the I.D. of the column, sent me out to reconnoitre. I was away for nearly three days and succeeded in getting behind the enemy's advanced position and was able to bring back useful information.

CHAPTER XXX

CONCLUSIONS

MY further ambition was to compile a map of the country within a radius of forty miles in front of us, for we would soon have to advance over it and it was shown on our military maps as almost a blank. At the Officers' Mess I had heard our General complaining bitterly of the lack of a proper map, so I determined to make one as soon as possible. The General was a man of great personality and one whom it was a pleasure to serve and I determined I would not rest until I had that map completed to hand him.

One day I returned from a patrol to find that from some source or other information had been received that the German main position, Mhambia, was evacuated and an old comrade of mine, Victor Dunman, also of the E.A.M.R. and now a Lieutenant in the K.A.R., was just starting out with a party of fifty askaris to investigate. I happened that very day to have spied on Mhambia from a distance and besides brought back a deserter who claimed that he had that very morning ground grain for an immense German army which was holding the place. Major Clifford Hill, who was always greatly interested in Intelligence work, had dropped into the I.D. banda, so I asked him to question the native again to make sure. The deserter held out his hands palm upwards, saying dramatically in native fashion :—

" You see these hands with the blisters on them ? This very morning they were pounding up grain for the German army and the askaris are many."

Major Hill immediately took the news to the O.C. K.A.R., and Duncan was spared a pretty warm reception, which he would most certainly have got had he walked into the supposed deserted camp and I was glad to feel that my timely arrival had not only possibly saved an old comrade's life, but perhaps most of his little force as well. Poor old Duncan, however, was destined it seemed to end his days at Mhambia, for some weeks later when our forces attacked he received his death wound there.

For another week I worked on the map and scouted down as far as the neighbourhood of Kihundu and Marentende for information. The map not only showed, all water-holes, roads and enemy positions, but the distance from each place was marked off in hour marches, it being the custom of the local natives to describe distances in hour or day marches as the case might be.

When the first draft was finished I checked and rechecked the work by information from different natives, until I was quite sure it was as near correct as possible under the circumstances. On my way back we were cautiously picking our way along in the neighbourhood of Mpingo, a place some six miles behind Mhambia, when I suddenly noticed before me a German white officer with a party of askaris not much larger than my own. They were marching along unconcernedly, feeling safe no doubt in their own neighbourhood, so I determined to follow them, for an opportunity might occur for an ambush. After going about a mile through country well suited for the purpose, I noticed one of the men who had been limping, now lagging farther and farther behind. At last he sat down to draw a thorn from his foot and as his companions drew out of sight we quickly surrounded and captured him, without firing a shot. He was a Wanyamwezi and as my orderly, Hamis, was also of the same tribe, I told him to take charge of the prisoner, treat him kindly and get all the information he could out of him.

When the man told his story I realized how lucky a capture it was, as far as Intelligence information went, for he was from Von Lettow's own especial company and told us that the German General had arrived with reinforcements that day.

This information was of the greatest importance as it had been generally understood by our Intelligence that Von Lettow was making towards the Lindi front and his arrival here might make all the difference to future operations.

That night we hid in a patch of scrub about six miles from our camp, meaning to make an early start and arrive in camp for breakfast, but all through the night I lay shivering with ague or burning with fever—the old complaint—and it was not until the afternoon that I staggered into camp. I handed in the prisoner, completed map and a statement of my information to my O.C. and these were my last services in the East African Campaign.

For some days I lay very ill in my banda. Then I had to go to hospital. I remember little of the journey to the coast. I was kept at Kilwa base hospital for a month, but getting no better was sent on to Dar-es-Salaam, where I stayed for some time until I became a little better. I was then sent back to my home in the highlands of East Africa to recuperate, and eventually was making my way to the front again, which had now moved down to Portuguese territory, when I had a relapse and became so ill that I had to be sent back to Dar-es-Salaam. The doctor who was attending me said I was of no further use for the front, and I certainly did not feel any good to anybody, so I applied for a discharge on medical grounds, explaining that when I fully recovered my health, if the war was not over, I would join up again, and on these grounds my discharge was granted.

Meanwhile our forces pursued the Germans across the Rovuma River into Portuguese territory, where the enemy found themselves in clover, for the cruelly oppressed natives of Portuguese East Africa welcomed them as Heaven-sent deliverers, and the cunning German leader was not slow to take full advantage of the situation.

Our Intelligence Department, I was told, had a particularly difficult time and realized how easy their work had been made for them in German East Africa, with the local natives on our side. Now the tables were completely turned, for to these natives the British were the friends and brothers of the

Portuguese, a loathsome pest of bloodsuckers to be wiped off the face of the earth. To please the natives more, the Germans made a point of methodically burning down every Portuguese fortress which they came upon.

When Von Lettow with his forces first crossed the Rovuma into Portuguese territory he was sorely pressed from shortage of ammunition, but soon fitted himself out afresh from the supplies of our timid allies, who had been collecting great stores of the sinews of war at their advanced posts, but fled when the Germans approached on the scene, leaving them in full possession. This was a sad blow for us, for it enabled our enemy to prolong the campaign for months. However, in time they were driven from Portuguese territory by our pursuing forces and took refuge in a remote part of Northern Rhodesia, where their leader surrendered to the British on Armistice Day.

Our other allies in the East African Campaign were the Belgians, who in 1916 with their fierce askaris recruited often from half-tamed cannibal tribes, came down on the south-west end of German East Africa, driving the enemy before them, much in the same way as we had been doing, until they eventually linked up with our forces at Tabora.

Thus, the Germans in East Africa who started the aggression by crossing the border of British East Africa in 1914, were eventually, with enormous cost and loss of many lives, not only driven from their own country, but right through the neighbouring Portuguese territory as well, where they fled into the wilds of North-western Rhodesia, over a hundred miles from their own colony.

In May, 1919, the conquered territory was mandated to three powers ; Great Britain took over the larger portion, the Belgians took over the beautiful highland cattle country of Urindi and Ruanda in the north-western part of the territory and a small portion at the coast, known as the Kionga Triangle, was given to the Portuguese.

The cost of the campaign to Great Britain alone was over £72,000,000. It seems difficult for one who fought and struggled in the campaign to see what claim Germany can possibly have in wanting Tanganyika Territory back. Moreover, we all know the Germans' aptitude for militarizing the African native and it would need but capital and enterprise to turn the teeming millions of Tanganyika's peaceful population into an efficient machine of destruction, instead of an efficient machine of production, which the British Administration and the various Missions in the mandated territory are striving to achieve. Should the Colony be returned and the Germans start to create this machine of destruction, hitherto peaceful neighbours, the British, the Belgians and the Portuguese, must likewise in defence create their machines of destruction, as they all have raw material (man power) in abundance, equal or even in some cases better than that found in Tanganyika, with results which it would take those with far greater insight than myself to forecast. But even the humblest traveller in Africa would readily realize that it would be the end of the African's welfare, his home

life and natural occupation of tilling the land,
tending his cattle and raising his family and slowly
educating himself and so improving his lot in this
world.   And that after all, is the responsibility of
those who take over slices of Africa.

THE END

INDEX